THE *New England Diner* COOKBOOK

Classic and Creative Recipes from the Finest Roadside Eateries

Mike Urban

The Countryman Press

Woodstock, Vermont

Library of Congress Cataloging-in-Publication Data
Urban, Mike, author.
   The New England diner cookbook / Mike Urban.
      pages cm
   Includes index.
   ISBN 978-1-58157-179-0 (pbk.)
   1. Cooking, American—New England style. 2. Diners (Restaurants)—New England. I. Title.

   TX715.2.N48U73 2014
   647.950974--dc23

                                        2013049169

Photographs © Mike Urban unless otherwise specified

Book design and composition by Vicky Shea, Ponderosa Pine Design

Published by The Countryman Press, P.O. Box 748, Woodstock, VT 05091

Distributed by W. W. Norton & Company, Inc., 500 Fifth Avenue, New York, NY 10110

Printed in the United States of America by Versa Press, Peoria, Illinois.

The New England Diner Cookbook

ISBN 978-1-58157-179-0

10 9 8 7 6 5 4 3 2 1

Photo credits:

Page 2: iStockphoto.com/nickfree. *Page 6: Pancakes with syrup, upper left:* Shutterstock.com/Marie C Fields; *lower right:* Eric Kelly (Blue Plate Diner). *Page 7: pancakes:* Courtesy of Laurel Diner. *Page 8:* Eric Kelly (Blue Plate Diner). *Page 13:* Janet Picard. *Page 22:* Janet Picard. *Page 25:* Courtesy of Laurel Diner. *Page 40:* Courtesy of Sonny's Blue Benn Diner. *Page 41:* Courtesy of Seaplane Diner. *Page 46:* Courtesy of Seaplane Diner. *Page 47:* Courtesy of Laurel Diner. *Page 48:* Shutterstock.com/Igor Dutina. Page 49: Shutterstock.com/Joy Brown. *Page 52:* Eric Kelly (Blue Plate Diner). *Page 58:* Shutterstock.com/BW Folsom. *Page 63:* Paul Joseph/ Wikimedia Commons. *Page 66:* Shutterstock.com/Joshua Resnick. *Page 69:* Shutterstock.com/littleny. *Page 73:* Shutterstock.com/ MSPhotographic. *Page 79:* Shutterstock.com/Elena Shashkina. *Page 81:* Eric Kelly (Blue Plate Diner). *Page 90:* Shutterstock.com/ MSPhotographic. *Page 93:* Shutterstock.com/Charles Brutlag. *Page 105:* Courtesy of Seaplane Diner. *Page 117:* Shutterstock.com/ tacar. *Page 119:* Eric Kelly (Blue Plate Diner). *Page 121:* Eric Kelly (Blue Plate Diner). *Page 126:* Shutterstock.com/Joe Gough. *Page 131:* Eric Kelly (Blue Plate Diner). *Page 133:* Eric Kelly (Blue Plate Diner). *Page 139:* Shutterstock.com/Brent Hofacker. *Page 141:* Shutterstock.com/hd Connelly. *Page 151:* Courtesy of Cadco Ltd. *Page 157:* Eric Kelly (Blue Plate Diner). *Page 159:* Shutterstock. com/Hannamariah. *Page 160:* Courtesy of A1 Diner. *Page 165:* Courtesy of Moody's Diner. *Page 170:* Shutterstock.com/Martin Gardeazabal. *Page 174:* Shutterstock.com/A_Lein. *Page 177:* Shutterstock.com/Jamie Rogers. *Page 186:* Sharon from Sydney, Australia/Wikimedia Commons. *Page 187:* Courtesy of Moody's Diner. *Page 189:* Courtesy of Moody's Diner. *Page 200*: Janet Picard. *Page 204:* Courtesy of Moody's Diner. *Page 205:* Shutterstock.com/Brent Hofacker. *Page 210:* Courtesy of A1 Diner. *Page 216:* Shutterstock.com/MSPhotographic.

THE *New England Diner* COOKBOOK

To my siblings—
Dave, Nancy, and Liz

Contents

Introduction

Diner food is every bit as American as baseball, jazz, and Norman Rockwell. Created by a culture of hard-working people with hearty appetites, a yearning for comfort food, and a need for affordable prices, this cuisine is every bit as red, white, and blue as any other regional American cooking, and New England is the region where diners and diner food were born.

Diners first appeared as all-night eateries in the late 1800s in places like Providence, Rhode Island, and other industrialized cities. Originally called "lunch wagons," these cafes on wheels catered to third-shift factory workers, newspapermen, and other night owls. The food served up was hearty, satisfying, and inexpensive, and it was prepared quickly for people on the go. In the early to mid-1900s, diner chefs put lots of time and love into developing their unique brand of homemade dishes, such as meat loaf, mac and cheese, chili, corned beef hash, homefries, and burgers, and it's this distinctively American brand of cuisine that's celebrated in this book.

The New England Diner Cookbook captures the essence of diner cuisine through more than 100 recipes from some 25 diners. In addition,

The A1 Diner, Gardiner, Maine.

there are short features describing some of the best New England diners to visit, and interesting sidebars explain how to prepare diner food and where to learn more about diner culture while mastering the craft of diner cookery at home.

The book opens with an array of breakfast recipes, many of which will be familiar and some that may come as a complete surprise. From omelets to pancakes and waffles to several different types of French toast and eggs Benedict, there's plenty to try out here for that first meal of the day.

"Soups, Chowders, and Chilies" features nearly a dozen recipes from this often overlooked category of diner fare. Some of New England's best chowders come from diners, many of them seafood-based, while others draw their ingredients from the garden. Chili is another New England diner favorite, and though it's a dish more often associated with the American Southwest, there are plenty of tasty, spicy versions to be found in the Northeastern corner of the country as well.

The heart of the book lies in the "Diner Classics" chapter, with its calorie-heavy comfort foods like meat loaf (several different versions), beef stew, New England boiled dinner, and chicken pot pie. Be sure to note the variations on some of the recipes. Subtle differences in ingredients and cooking methods can help turn a picky eater into an avid diner food fan. Have fun trying out these recipes, which offer broad latitude to improvise on ingredients, proportions, and cooking techniques.

Seafood isn't usually the first thing that comes to mind when thinking of diners and diner food, but New England's proximity to some of the best, most diverse fisheries in the world helps dress up the region's diner menus with some amazing dishes. Diner seafood boasts unique lobster, clam, and scallop dishes, and there are plenty of tasty, healthy finned-fish recipes included here too. From lobster pie to beer-steamed clams to New England cod cakes, this chapter is full of pleasant seafood surprises.

Several of New England's more progressive, experimental diners have menus and specials that greatly expand the traditional meaning of diner food. From Neapolitan-like American chop suey to grilled cheese with lobster and brie to lamb burgers laced with cilantro and goat cheese, the recipes in this chapter offer some surprising entrées and side dishes that greatly expand the palette of diner recipe choices.

Speaking of side dishes, this is another culinary corner where New England diners really shine. Hash of various types, homefries, and seafood-laced fritters are some of the sides found in nearly every diner in the region, and there are several easy-to-follow recipes from which to choose.

No diner meal is complete without some home-made dessert and a cup of fresh-brewed coffee. The "Diner Desserts" chapter contains 16 recipe ideas for everything from Indian Pudding to Grape Nut Pudding to bread pudding, as well as cookies, whoopie pies, brownies, and more.

Fresh-baked pie is synonymous with diner food—especially in New England, where a handful of diners stake their reputations on their amazing pie offerings. From Moody's Four Berry Pie to the Agawam Diner's Coconut Cream Pie, there are several rich and rewarding recipes to try in this chapter. In addition, many New England diner owners rise well before sunrise to bake their own bread, muffins, and cakes, showing them off in glass display cases by the counter; some of their best baking recipes are also included here.

New England diner food is so much more than burgers, fries, and shakes, and the amazing culinary variety offered by New England's finest diners comes to life in the recipes, pictures, and stories herein. Give some of these recipes a try, then hit the road and check out the real thing at the New England diners of your choice.

Breakfast Fare

Nothing is finer than breakfast at a diner. These uniquely American eateries were made for the morning meal. Most diners are open by 6 am or earlier, and that's when many of them do most of their business.

Beginning in the early 1900s, a whole breakfast cuisine sprang from the collective menus of diners everywhere. Bacon, eggs, sausage, pancakes, omelets, hash, waffles, French toast—all these platters of comfort food were heaven to workers on their way to a long day on the job or a welcome reward after coming off the third shift.

In today's New England diners, you're likely to discover some pretty innovative variations on standard American breakfast themes. In this chapter you'll find a distinctively Irish take on the omelet; French toast dishes stuffed with anything from cream cheese to lemon-flavored ricotta; some real, old-fashioned doughnut recipes from a couple of diners that still make their own; and some fancy brunch-style eggs Benedict dishes bathed in rich, creamy hollandaise sauce.

Some of these recipes will challenge your kitchen skills, but many have been selected for their simplicity and for their straightforward, honest approaches to that first meal of the day. After trying a number of the French toast recipes in this chapter, you'll never look at the egg-dipped bread dish in quite the same way. Enjoy!

DUBLINER OMELET

Omelets are one of the main attractions at O'Rourke's, one of the finest diners in all of New England. At any given time, chef/owner Brian O'Rourke has at least 20 different types on the menu, virtually all of which are his original creations. Perhaps the most popular omelet at O'Rourke's is the Dubliner, an eggs, bacon, hash, and cheese dish that has a distinctively Irish flavor, with its specialty Irish bacon, corned beef hash, Irish butter, and cheddar cheese. This omelet is usually served at the diner with Fingerlings (see page 150), Irish Soda Bread (see page 214), and Raspberry Jam (see page 215) on the side.

2   slices Irish bacon

2   tablespoons vegetable shortening or butter (¼ stick, 1 ounce; Irish butter is recommended and available in many grocery stores), divided

½   cup Corned Beef Hash (see page 140)

3   medium eggs

1–2   cups grated cheddar cheese

Salt and pepper to taste

1. Cook the Irish bacon in a skillet. Remove the bacon and set on a paper towel to drain. Add 1 tablespoon of shortening or butter to the skillet. Allow it to melt, then add the corned beef hash. Cook until browned, then turn off the heat.

2. In a bowl, whisk the eggs thoroughly. In a second pan, melt 1 tablespoon of butter over medium heat, then pour in the eggs. When the eggs begin to cook, place the browned corned beef hash across the middle of the eggs. (Envision your omelet being a trifold with your ingredients in the center.) Sprinkle on the cheddar cheese and let it melt.

3. When the eggs are cooked, fold each edge of the omelet over the hash. Flip the omelet over so that the seam is on the bottom. Cook a minute more. Avoid overcooking—the inside should stay juicy. Add salt and pepper to taste and top with the Irish bacon. Serves 1.

HOMEMADE DOUGHNUTS

SONNY'S BLUE BENN DINER, BENNINGTON, VT

The best diners often have fresh doughnuts under glass behind the counter or by the cash register to tempt customers with one last taste treat before settling up. Rare is the diner that still makes its own doughnuts, and Sonny's Blue Benn is one of them. Owner Sonny Monroe has been cooking up batches for his customers first thing in the morning for years, and with this recipe you can give it a try at home. Who knows—maybe it'll inspire you to open your own diner or doughnut shop some day!

1	tablespoon salt
¼	teaspoon nutmeg
1	cup sugar
3	eggs
3½	cups all-purpose flour
4	teaspoons baking powder
¾	cup buttermilk
1–2	cups shortening
½	teaspoon cinnamon (optional)

1. In a mixing bowl, combine salt, nutmeg, sugar, and eggs and mix well. Add the flour and baking powder. Gradually blend the buttermilk into the mixture to make dough.

2. Roll out the dough into ½-inch slices and cut with a doughnut cutter. Fry in a deep fryer or heavy skillet with at least an inch of shortening in it. The oil should be heated to 350°F. Cook the doughnuts evenly on each side until golden brown and firm. Place on paper towels to drain, and sprinkle with cinnamon. Makes about 12 doughnuts.

(As an afterthought, a member of the waitstaff at the Blue Benn came up with an idea for a doughnut treat in the afternoon: Take a doughnut, slice it in half, place it on a grill or in a pan with some butter for a few minutes, then serve it with a scoop of vanilla ice cream on top or on the side. Sort of a doughnut à la mode.)

DOTTIE'S HOMEMADE BUTTERMILK PANCAKES

DOTTIE'S DINER, WOODBURY, CT

There's probably no better place to get real, homemade pancakes than at a diner, where they're expertly prepared on a large, gas-fired griddle that cooks them evenly and consistently. Dottie's buttermilk pancakes also come out nicely on the home griddle or frypan, and the brown sugar gives them an added exotic sweetness that complements whatever type of syrup you decide to pour over them.

- 5 cups all-purpose flour
- ¾ cup brown sugar
- 3 tablespoons baking powder
- ¾ tablespoons baking soda
- ½ tablespoon salt
- 5 eggs
- ½ cup (1 stick, 4 ounces) butter, melted
- 2 teaspoons vanilla extract
- 1 quart buttermilk

1. Mix the flour, brown sugar, baking powder, baking soda, and salt in a large bowl. In a separate bowl, combine the eggs, melted butter, vanilla, and buttermilk. Beat together, then add to the dry ingredients. Stir together only until the dry ingredients are moist. Let stand for several minutes.

2. Ladle the batter onto a heated, oiled griddle or pan. Flip each pancake when the top is bubbly and the underside is brown and firm enough to be flipped without splattering. Makes 15–20 pancakes.

LEMON RICOTTA-STUFFED FRENCH TOAST WITH BLUEBERRY COMPOTE

JIGGER'S HILL AND HARBOUR DINER, EAST GREENWICH, RI

The title of this recipe is a mouthful in itself, but oh, what a mouthful! This wonderful French toast concoction comes from the recently refurbished Jigger's Hill and Harbour Diner, where the offerings tend to be a bit on the gourmet side, but where you may also still find good ol' diner food. This dish is fairly easy to prepare—just some mixing and little bit of cooking—and the payback is a good-looking, fine-tasting meal.

LEMON RICOTTA FILLING

2	cups ricotta cheese
4	tablespoons lemon zest
1	teaspoon lemon juice

FRENCH TOAST

2	eggs
1	tablespoon vanilla extract
4	pieces Texas toast

BLUEBERRY COMPOTE

1	cup water
1	cup sugar
2	cups blueberries
1	tablespoon lemon juice
2	tablespoons confectioners' sugar

1. To make the lemon ricotta filling, combine the ricotta cheese, lemon zest, and lemon juice in a bowl.

2. To make the blueberry compote, bring the water and sugar to a boil. Keep it boiling for 5 minutes, stirring occasionally. Add the blueberries, reduce to a simmer, and cook for 2 minutes. Add the lemon juice and remove from heat.

3. To make the French toast batter, whisk the eggs and vanilla together in a shallow bowl until well blended. Dip half the toast pieces into the batter, and lay them on a preheated griddle or skillet.

4. Spread the lemon ricotta filling onto the grilling toast pieces, then dip the remaining toast pieces into the batter and place them on top of each piece of toast on the griddle or skillet.

5. Flip each piece of toast over after a few minutes, and brown each French toast ricotta sandwich on both sides. Remove the sandwiches from the griddle or skillet, and cut each diagonally. Place the triangular French toast slices so that they overlap on the plate. Drizzle the blueberry compote over the top of each plate of toast, and dust with confectioners' sugar. Serves 2.

A Truly Extraordinary Diner

✕ 728 Main Street
Middletown, CT 06457

☎ 860-346-6101

ⓘ www.orourkesmiddletown.com

O'Rourke's Diner

Step into O'Rourke's in Middletown, Connecticut, grab a stool at the counter or a seat in one of the booths, sit back, and wait to be wowed by the amazing things that come out of the kitchen at this regionally and nationally famous eatery, which has had more than one life in its span of 70-plus years.

O'Rourke's first opened its doors in 1941, when John O'Rourke bought the wood-framed Dunn's Diner and began serving breakfast and lunch to the locals. In 1946, he replaced the diner with a chrome-and-glass Mountain View diner and continued cooking for another 30 years.

In 1977, John's nephew, Brian O'Rourke, and Brian's cousin John Sweeney purchased the diner, with Brian subsequently buying out John to become sole owner in 1985. Brian had been working at O'Rourke's since he was a kid in the late 1950s, and he developed a passion for playing around in the kitchen, experimenting with recipes and ingredients.

Tapping his Irish heritage, Brian began serving up dishes such as Irish Stew and omelets stuffed with corned beef hash, cabbage, Irish bacon, and Irish cheddar cheese. During the 1980s, he took sabbaticals to spend time cooking in kitchens in New Orleans, Ireland, and the Caribbean, which gave him a unique and evolving culinary perspective.

In 2006, the diner was gutted by fire and all but destroyed. The entire Middletown and nearby Wesleyan University communities rallied to support Brian, raising some $300,000 to help him rebuild and reopen, which he did a year and a half later. Few diners, or restaurants of any kind, have this sort of loyal, passionate following, but O'Rourke's Diner

O'Rourke's was completely remodeled after a fire gutted it in 2006.

is such a focal point of downtown Middletown life that its rising from the ashes only served to affirm its longtime importance to the community.

Today, O'Rourke's is a place of never-ending surprises, where Brian comes up with new specials almost daily, depending on what he finds in the larder when he arrives in the morning. There is an extensive menu of regular items, such as the Dubliner Omelet (see page 15), Banana Bread French Toast, Eggs Mornay, and Brian's Rueben Sandwich. O'Rourke's is also one of the few places anywhere that serves steamed cheeseburgers, a central Connecticut specialty, which are made in a custom-built steamer in which freshly ground beef and slabs of Irish cheddar cheese are given a super-hot sauna until cooked and melted to perfection.

O'Rourke's Diner is an icon on Main Street in Middletown, Connecticut.

There's always something baking at O'Rourke's, be it loaves of bread, muffins, biscuits, cookies, or other baked goods. Upon being seated at the diner, patrons are treated to a small plate of bread samples that were cooked up that day. There's a never-ending variety of things coming out of Brian's ovens, and during the holidays, it's a great place to put in an order for wonderful baked goods to take home with you.

Wesleyan University Press has contracted with Brian to publish *Breakfast at O'Rourke's,* a cookbook that contains 73 recipes for baked goods, omelets, French toasts, frittatas, quiches, sauces, side dishes, and more. A concluding chapter in the book combines many of the 73 recipes into 23 inspired diner breakfasts that will leave your family and guests wowed and grateful. Written in a simple, easy-to-follow style, the book is a godsend for those who believe that breakfast is the best meal of the day.

There's no way to describe what specials might await you when you visit O'Rourke's on any given day. Brian frequently steps out of the kitchen and visits his diners throughout the day, handing out small samples from his latest tinkerings in the kitchen. Ask him what he recommends to order, and listen closely to what he says. It's guaranteed you won't be disappointed. We can only hope that this extraordinary diner owner and chef keeps it up for many years to come.

Chef/owner Brian O'Rourke, working his magic at the stove.

CAJUN BREAKFAST SKILLET

CHELSEA ROYAL DINER, WEST BRATTLEBORO, VT

This mélange of meat and veg is one of the most popular breakfast dishes at southern Vermont's Chelsea Royal Diner. It has a little bit of everything in it, and though it may be Cajun in its seasonings only, it's a hearty and satisfying way to start your day.

Royal Diner by Janet Picard

1	pound ground bulk sweet Italian sausage
1	tablespoon fresh garlic, minced
2–3	tablespoons Cajun seasoning, divided
1	small green bell pepper, cut into thin strips
1	small red bell pepper, cut into thin strips
½	onion, cut into thin strips
1½	pounds firm-cooked, diced potatoes (leftover baked potatoes work fine)
8	eggs
4	tablespoons (½ stick, 2 ounces) butter, divided
1	cup grated cheddar cheese (Vermont cheddar is, of course, preferred)

1. Preheat the oven to 350°F. In a cast-iron skillet, melt half the butter and cook the Italian sausage, garlic, half the Cajun seasoning, the bell peppers, and the onion together. When the sausage is cooked thoroughly and the veggies are tender, add the cooked, diced potatoes and blend gently with a spoon. Add more Cajun seasoning to taste.

2. Separate the meat-and-veg mixture into four individual-size ovenproof bowls or dishes. Place them in the preheated oven to keep them warm.

3. Cook the eggs over easy two at a time in a skillet with the remainder of the butter, and place the eggs on top of the mixture-filled bowls. Sprinkle cheddar cheese on top of each one, and place them back in the oven until the cheese is melted. Serves 4.

SUN-DRIED TOMATO, CARAMELIZED ONION, AND FETA CHEESE OMELET

MODERN DINER, PAWTUCKET, RI

According to the Modern Diner's warm-hearted, energetic owner, Nick Demou, this is one of the most popular items on the menu. He stresses that the better the sun-dried tomatoes, the tastier the omelet. This seems obvious, but it's important enough that he verbally underlined this point several times while dictating the recipe.

The other secret to this omelet's success is the sort of reverse order in which it's made—by pouring the beaten eggs over the caramelized onions so the onions continue to cook on the outside of the omelet, instead of folding them inside, as most omelet makers do with their ingredients. Try making this at home, then beat a path to the Modern to try the real thing.

2	eggs
4	tablespoons extra virgin olive oil, divided
4	sun-dried tomatoes
½	red onion, diced
2	tablespoons feta cheese, crumbled

1. Beat the eggs and 2 tablespoons of the olive oil in a small bowl. Pour the other 2 tablespoons of olive oil onto a griddle or into an omelet or other pan and warm under medium heat. When warmed through, add the red onions and sauté until caramelized.

2. Pour the egg and olive oil mixture over the red onions and cook until the underside is firm. Place the sun-dried tomatoes and feta cheese on top, fold the firmed-up eggs in half to form an omelet, then cook briefly, turning the omelet over in the pan once, until the feta cheese softens and melts inside. Serves 1.

CINNAMON ROLL FRENCH TOAST

LAUREL DINER, SOUTHBURY, CT

Here's a unique twist on the French toast theme: Take a good-size cinnamon bun, cut it in half lengthwise, and cook it up as if it's French toast. As Stephanie Homick, co-owner of the Laurel Diner, says, "It's truly decadent!"

2	tablespoons (¼ stick, 1 ounce) butter
1	egg
¼	cup milk
	Hint of vanilla extract
1	large cinnamon roll, cut in half lengthwise
	Fresh strawberries (raspberries and bananas are worthy substitutes)
	Whipped cream

1. Heat a skillet or griddle to medium-high heat, then add the butter and melt.

2. To make the French toast batter, whisk the egg, milk, and vanilla together in a shallow bowl until well blended. Take the two split pieces of cinnamon roll and dip the interior sides of the roll into the batter.

3. Place the interior sides of the roll onto the heated, buttered skillet or griddle. Cook until golden brown, then flip over onto the sugary, glazed sides until crisp. Remove from the heat and top with fresh fruit and whipped cream. Serves 1.

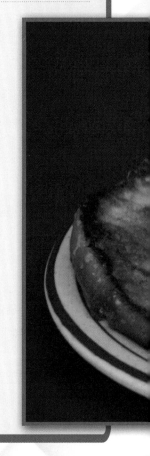

On Making a Great Omelet

Brian O'Rourke, owner of O'Rourke's Diner in Middletown, Connecticut, knows a thing or two about making omelets. Here's an excerpt from his forthcoming cookbook, *Breakfast at O'Rourke's*, in which he dishes on a few things he's learned over the years, after having mixed, folded, and flipped tens of thousands of omelets:

There are many keys to making a great omelet. If you use butter to grease your pan, you will have a good omelet, but if you use Irish butter, then you will have a better omelet. (Irish butter has a higher concentration of butter fat and can be found in most grocery stores.) The temperature of the pan makes a difference as well as the quality and temperature of your eggs. Using room temperature eggs makes a better omelet, and I suggest letting eggs sit on the counter for about two hours before you prepare the dish. Once you master a basic omelet, you can then experiment with different ingredients and flavors. Some prefer raw ingredients in their omelet while others like to sauté their ingredients and then add them. Condiments and sauces are also a great way to alter the appearance, and taste, of your basic omelets.

PUMPKIN PANCAKES WITH CARAMELIZED BANANAS, PECANS, AND RAISINS

BLUE PLATE DINER, MIDDLETOWN, RI

This fancy breakfast dish appears on the menu at the Blue Plate in autumn, when flavors like pumpkin, cinnamon, and ginger are particularly appealing. Don't be put off by the extensive ingredients list—most of the work, other than cooking the pancakes and heating up the sauce, involves mixing ingredients in bowls. All the mixing and blending is rewarded with a truly gourmet stack of pancakes.

PANCAKES

1½ cups milk

1 cup pumpkin puree

1 egg

2 tablespoons canola oil

2 tablespoons vinegar

2 cups all-purpose flour

3 tablespoons light brown sugar

2 teaspoons baking powder

2 teaspoons baking soda

1 teaspoon ground allspice

1 teaspoon cinnamon

½ teaspoon ground ginger

½ teaspoon salt

SAUCE

½ cup brown sugar

2 tablespoons (¼ stick, 1 ounce) butter, melted

1 banana, peeled and sliced into ¼-inch-thick rounds

¼ cup raisins

¼ cup pecans

1. To make the pancakes, mix together the milk, pumpkin, egg, oil, and vinegar in a bowl.

2. In a separate bowl, combine the flour, brown sugar, baking powder, baking soda, allspice, cinnamon, ginger, and salt. Slowly stir into the pumpkin mixture, just enough to combine.

3. Onto a lightly oiled griddle, about 350°F, scoop about ¼ of the mixture for each pancake. Cook for 60–90 seconds on each side or until the sides start to bubble. Look for a light golden brown and fluffy pancake.

The Blue Plate Diner's full-service bar and waiting area.

4. To make the sauce, heat the butter in a heavy saucepan and melt. Add the brown sugar and melt, then add the banana, raisins, and pecans. Pour over the pancakes, and serve hot. Make sure that the sugar and butter mixture does not get overheated, or it will separate. Makes 4 large pancakes.

CHOURIÇO AND POTATO EGGS BENEDICT

JIGGER'S HILL AND HARBOUR DINER, EAST GREENWICH, RI

Chouriço (pronounced shore-EEEZ) is a spicy Portuguese sausage similar to Mexican chorizo, and it's quite common in many diners throughout New England, especially in communities where Portuguese immigrants have settled over the years. It's a very versatile breakfast meat, finding its way into many egg dishes and also served as a side instead of bacon, sausage, or ham. This chouriço diner dish is more elaborate than others, but it's also a standout in its complexity of flavors and its overall ability to please family and friends.

HOLLANDAISE SAUCE

4	egg yolks
3	tablespoons freshly squeezed lemon juice
	Pinch of pepper
	Dash of Worcestershire sauce
1	tablespoon water
1	cup (2 sticks, 8 ounces) butter, melted
¼	teaspoon salt

EGGS BENEDICT

2	English muffins, split in half
½	pound chouriço sausage, chopped into ½-inch cubes
½	medium onion, chopped
½	green bell pepper, diced
	Homefries (using red potatoes; see pages 141, 152)
4	eggs

1. To make the hollandaise sauce, put water in the bottom of a double boiler and bring it to a gentle, steaming simmer. Place the top portion of the double boiler over the warm water, and whisk in the yolks, lemon juice, pepper, Worcestershire sauce, and water. Slowly add the melted butter, then the salt, whisking constantly. If the hollandaise is too thick, add a teaspoon of warm water and whisk to the desired consistency. Remove the sauce from the heat and cover to keep warm.

2. To prepare the eggs Benedict, toast or grill the English muffins. Sauté the chouriço, onions, green peppers, and homefries in a skillet, then spoon onto the toasted muffins.

3. Poach the eggs and place one on top of each muffin. Top each serving with hollandaise sauce. Serves 2.

RASPBERRY CRUNCH FRENCH TOAST

SONNY'S BLUE BENN DINER, BENNINGTON, VT

This breakfast specialty was created by the Blue Benn's Bill Walsh. It brings together an unlikely quartet of breakfast staples—cornflakes, raspberries, raspberry jam, and cream cheese—along with several other tasty ingredients to make the crunchiest French toast you'll ever have.

SYRUP

3	cups frozen raspberries
2	cups sugar
1½	cups water, divided
3	cups raspberry jam
2	tablespoons corn starch

FROSTING

⅓	cup cream cheese
1	tablespoon vanilla extract

TOAST

4	eggs
⅔	cup milk
1	medium box cornflakes
8–10	bread slices
1	cup confectioners' sugar
	Butter (enough for frying)

1. To make the syrup, place the raspberries, sugar, and half the water in a saucepan. Bring to a boil, reduce to a simmer, and stir. Add the jam and keep stirring. Lower the heat further and continue stirring. Mix the corn starch with the rest of the water in a small bowl, add to the syrup to thicken it slightly, then turn off the heat.

2. To make a smooth frosting, mix the cream cheese, vanilla, and confectioners' sugar with an electric mixer. Add a tablespoon of raspberry syrup to color it, and keep the frosting at room temperature.

3. To make the batter, whisk the eggs and milk together in a shallow bowl until well blended. Then grind the cornflakes coarsely in a food processor and place in another bowl.

4. Dip the bread slices into the batter, then into the cornflakes, thoroughly covering both sides. Place the slices on a heated, buttered griddle or skillet and cook, turning once, until golden brown on both sides. Remove from heat, and cut each slice in half. Garnish each piece with frosting, syrup, and confectioners' sugar. Serves 4.

MONKEY TOAST

PALACE DINER, BIDDEFORD, ME

The Palace Diner's Monkey Toast mixes the health boost that comes from bananas with the indulgence of butter, sugar, caramel sauce, dark chocolate, and whipped cream. This seemingly conflicting mash-up of nutritional do's and don'ts comes together beautifully in the form of a French toast dish that's as pretty to look at as it is delicious to eat.

6 eggs	Confectioners' sugar
¼ cup vanilla extract	Small jar caramel sauce
6 slices Texas toast	½ cup dark chocolate, shaved
2 tablespoons (¼ stick, 1 ounce) butter	4 tablespoons whipped cream
2 bananas, peeled and sliced lengthwise	

1. Preheat and butter a griddle or heavy skillet over medium heat.

2. To make the batter, beat the eggs in a large bowl. Add the vanilla and mix well. Quickly dredge the Texas toast slices in the batter, making sure the slices don't get soaked in the egg and vanilla.

3. After dredging, immediately place the toast slices on the preheated griddle or skillet. Cook until golden brown on the underside, about 2–3 minutes. Flip the toast slices and brown on the other side.

4. At the same time, melt the butter in a skillet, and carefully brown the split bananas in the butter, gently turning them over once. The bananas should be soft but not falling apart.

5. Stack the browned toast slices, three to a plate, in a crisscross pattern. Butter the top piece gently, so as not to crush the stack. Sprinkle with confectioners' sugar, then add the cooked banana slices, two per stack. Drizzle caramel sauce over the entire stack, sprinkle some shaved chocolate on top, and place a generous dollop of whipped cream on the side. Serves 2.

The Vermont Diner with a Vegetarian Twist

✕ 314 North Street
Bennington, VT 05201

☎ 802-442-5140

Sonny's Blue Benn Diner

When motoring north on US 7 out of the town of Bennington, Vermont, on the way to Bennington College, there's a bend in the road to the northwest. On the west side of that bend sits Sonny's Blue Benn Diner, immediately recognizable by its twin blue awnings and its stainless steel railcar-like exterior. This is a must-stop for any diner lover, vegetarian, or dyed-in-the-wool fan of authentic mid-twentieth-century Americana.

This Silk City–design diner was manufactured in the late 1940s in Paterson, New Jersey, then shipped to Bennington, where it was assembled in 1948 on the same site it occupies today. (This is noteworthy, as many diners are picked up and moved at least once in their lifetimes, especially ones in relatively remote locations like the Blue Benn's.)

In 1974, husband and wife Sonny and Marylou Monroe purchased the diner and started operating it as a family business. Over time, they started expanding their menu with healthy alternatives to their standard diner fare, especially in the form of vegetarian offerings. This put them a bit ahead of the culinary curve, but they found a willing audience in Vermont and from Bennington College in particular.

Today, Blue Benn's menu is about an even split between meat and potatoes and meatless dishes from around the world. Sonny's Falafel was a pioneering addition that caught on right away, and it has been followed by such Blue Benn mainstays as Veggie Lasagna, a shiitake mushroom and broccoli stir-fry, and a south-of-the-border Veggie Enchilada Platter.

The sheer size of the menu belies the physical dimensions of the place, which can seat around 40

Veggie enchiladas, one of many vegetarian dishes at Sonny's.

The posted specials almost outnumber the menu items at Sonny's Blue Benn Diner.

customers. (Yes, lines are common on weekends and in the summer.) There are dozens of items on the menu, including some amazing breakfast treats, such as Garden Scrambled, Banana Walnut Pancakes, and a monstrous Breakfast Burrito.

In addition, the walls behind the counter are covered with several dozen plastic-covered sheets of colored paper, each advertising a different special. For adventurous diners, there's no need to even read the regular menu; just feast your eyes on all the unusual and enticing dish descriptions hanging on the wall and order away.

Sonny and Marylou have not lost sight of the fact that their establishment is first and foremost a diner. They still serve up plenty of meat loaf, macaroni and cheese, pot roast, and grilled liver and onions. Their daughter, Lisa, has been increasingly involved in the business, and it appears that the happy Monroe vibe that makes this place so special will live on for quite some time.

COFFEE CAKE

DOTTIE'S DINER, WOODBURY, CT

Dottie's owners, Dorie and Ken Sperry, bake up this fresh coffee cake every morning and set it on a pastry stand next to the cash register by the door. Dottie's version is rich, dense, and flavorful—a more real, down-to-earth coffee cake than the over-iced monstrosities you find in supermarket bakery aisles.

TOPPING

1½	cups brown sugar
1½	cups walnuts, finely chopped (a food processor is helpful with this)
6	tablespoons all-purpose flour
6	tablespoons (¾ stick, 3 ounces) butter, melted
1	tablespoon cinnamon

CAKE

3	cups all-purpose flour
1	tablespoon plus 2 teaspoons baking powder
1	teaspoon salt
2	eggs
1½	cups granulated sugar
⅔	cup (1⅓ sticks, 5½ ounces) butter, melted
1	cup milk
2	teaspoons vanilla extract

1. To make the topping, mix all ingredients in a bowl and set aside.

2. To make the cake, preheat the oven to 350°F. Mix the flour, baking powder, and salt in a large bowl and set aside. Beat the eggs until frothy, add the sugar, and mix. Pour in the melted butter and mix again. Add the milk and vanilla and mix some more. Transfer to the large bowl of dry ingredients and blend. Pour the batter into a greased 9 x 13-inch baking dish and carefully cover with the topping. Bake for 35 minutes or until a cake tester comes out clean.

LAUREL OMELET

LAUREL DINER, SOUTHBURY, CT

This is a fully loaded and very flavorful omelet that's got lots of fresh veggies in it. Depending on your appetite, you may use either two or three eggs. Be sure to adjust your other ingredients accordingly.

- 2 tablespoons (¼ stick, 1 ounce) butter, divided
- 1–2 sausage links, sliced into small pieces
- Fresh spinach
- Fresh mushrooms
- Roasted red peppers (fresh is best; jarred will suffice)
- 2–3 eggs
- Crumbled feta cheese

1. Preheat a pan or griddle, and melt half the butter in it. Cook the sausage slices until browned. Remove from the pan. Add the spinach, mushrooms, and roasted red peppers to the pan and sauté for 1–2 minutes. Remove and set aside.

2. In a bowl, beat the eggs until they're fluffy. Put the remaining butter in the pan or griddle until melted, then pour in the beaten eggs. Once the eggs are bubbling on the surface, lay on the sausage mixture and crumbled feta cheese.

3. Carefully fold over one half of the egg to form an omelet. Let it cook for a minute or so, but don't let it turn brown. Carefully flip the omelet over and finish cooking for another minute or so. Plate and garnish with any leftover cooked vegetables. Serves 1.

Southbury's Hash House

✕ 544 Main Street South
Southbury, CT 06488

☎ 203-264-8218

Laurel Diner

About half a mile from Southbury, Connecticut's snappy, modern central business district, with its well-planned contemporary colonial storefronts and low-rise office buildings, sits a modest, whitewashed, one-story stucco building on leafy Main Street South. This quiet setting is a great spot for the wonderful cuisine to be had at the Laurel Diner, and if you're a fan of corned beef hash, this place should be your nirvana.

There has been a diner at this location since 1949, and the various owners over the years seem to make a go of it for about 15 years or so before selling out to the next grill chef. Current owner Pete Homick, who bought the Laurel in 1997, has broken that spell. He and his wife, Stephanie, seem to be just hitting their stride and looking forward to many more years of happy, hard-working diner ownership.

Pete came to the business somewhat unprepared, with no real cooking skills and believing that he and his two business partners would be able to delegate much of the work to employees. When their cook staff didn't work out, Pete manned the griddle and taught himself the art of diner cookery, one dish at a time. In the nearly 20 years he's been in business (he bought out his two partners over time), Pete has developed a repertoire of breakfast and lunch dishes that has a line of eager customers snaking out the front door down to the street nearly every weekend.

What brings people to an old-school eatery in such a modern, progressive-looking town? Pete and Stephanie believe it begins with the ingredients. Everything they prepare at their diner is as fresh and as honest as it can be. Their eggs come from a local farm, and much of their produce is locally harvested, including seasonal items from the organic garden in their back yard at home.

Then there's the tried-and-true cooking techniques that Pete has developed over thousands of hours tending the diner's griddle, slowly

Laurel Diner owners Stephanie and Pete Homick.

honing his craft into the fine art it has become. For instance, he initially used canned corned beef hash but wasn't pleased with the results. He started blending in his own ingredients and developing his own unique recipe until he hit on the amazing hash that comes off his griddle today. (He wisely won't share the recipe.) Once or twice a week, he cooks his own 30-plus-pound brisket for use in the hash, along with carefully selected potatoes and finely chopped onions. Making the hash every day is a labor of love, but he's famous for this dish. Roadfood.com's Michael Stern has been singing its praises for years.

On the breakfast side of the menu, the most popular dish is the Daily Special, which consists of a generous helping of Pete's famous hash, two eggs cooked any style, homefries, and toast (get the cinnamon raisin toast—it's

The Laurel Diner's Daily Special, featuring corned beef hash.

from a local bakery). The Grilled Cinnamon Roll is also very popular, especially with the many kids who accompany their parents to this family-friendly eatery. The Cinnamon Raisin French Toast is an unusually sweet, batter-dipped concoction that cooks up to a crispy perfection on the griddle, as does the he-man-friendly French Toast Riddler Sandwich—two pieces of French toast with a sausage patty and slice of cheese in between.

Pancakes and waffles come in all sorts of wonderful permutations and daily specials, and the omelets are lovingly grilled to fluffy perfection throughout the day. Of particular note is the Laurel Omelet, with its fresh spinach and mushrooms, roasted red peppers, and crumbled feta cheese.

Lunch certainly doesn't play second fiddle to breakfast here. Handmade burgers (try the BBQ Bacon and Onion Ring Burger), foot-long Hummel hot dogs, a Rueben sandwich with real sauerkraut, and an authentic Monte Cristo sandwich made on the griddle are some of the most popular offerings. And there's another side dish that has made addicts out of some of the Laurel's regular customers: Pete's homemade, thin, crispy, buttery hash brown potatoes, available any time of day.

Aesthetically, the Laurel is white on white. In addition to its white exterior, the diner's interior (save for the burnt-red counter- and tabletops) is also a sea of white. The ceiling and walls are smooth panels of sheet metal with baked-on white enamel paint, onto which the Homicks write the daily specials in colorful, erasable marker ink. There's a boom box at one end of the counter, tuned to a local classic rock station, giving the place a friendly kitchen-like feel.

Pete and Stephanie and Stephanie's sister Bianca (the Homicks's go-to head waitress) have cast a wonderful spell over this quiet diner not far off I-84. Be sure to put it high on your list of places to dine any time you'll be passing through western Connecticut. Did I mention to be sure to try the hash?

A Window into Diner History

Culinary Arts Museum, Johnson & Wales University

315 Harborside Boulevard

Providence, RI 02905

401-598-2805

www.culinary.org

At Johnson & Wales University in Providence, Rhode Island, there's an excellent museum tucked away on its Harborside campus that's dedicated to the culinary arts. A major part of the museum's collection is a permanent exhibit of artifacts from diners past and present, with a special emphasis on New England diners.

The Rhode Island location for this window into the world of diners is fitting. The American diner traces its origins to horse-drawn lunch carts, which first appeared on the streets of Providence in the 1870s. One of these, the "night lunch wagon," as it was called, used to park across the street from the *Providence Journal* newspaper and serve hungry employees working all hours of the night, writing copy, setting type, running the presses, and delivering the papers. Theater-goers, factory workers, barflies, and other late-night types were also frequent and regular patrons. The city's diner history runs long and deep from the 1870s to the present.

The diner exhibit isn't just a handful of glass cases containing old spatulas, griddles, waffle irons, milk shake blenders, and other artifacts. It's a full-blown, walk-through, 4,000-square-foot diner experience with neon diner signs, mock diner counters and tables, even a fully restored diner—the Ever Ready Diner, a 1926 Worcester Lunch Car diner that operated in Providence until 1989 when it was donated to the museum.

Inside the Ever Ready you'll find a marble countertop, stools, original tile work on the floor and walls, a

The Culinary Arts Museum at Johnson & Wales University, home of the Diner Exhibit.

The entrance to the Diner Exhibit.

griddle, a classic coffee urn, period light fixtures, and numerous other authentic touches. A couple of manne-quins, one posing as counter help and the other as a customer, are in period clothing, adding to the realistic air of the place. All the interior stainless steel and chrome are polished to a high shine, and the trademark Worcester diner car's barrel-shaped ceiling caps off the classic diner look and feel. You'll find it hard not to sidle up and grab a stool in hopes of ordering up a cup of coffee and slice of pie or a hot meal.

Outside the Ever Ready is a small expanse of Formica-top tables and chrome-plated, red-padded chairs, grouped around a restored soda fountain with Hamilton Beach milk shake mixers and other vintage equipment on display. The original sign from Moody's Diner in Waldoboro, Maine, hangs on one wall, casting a warm, reddish neon glow over the entire scene.

Elsewhere in the exhibit are numerous historical photos of vintage diners and lunch carts and lots of informa-tive display boards explaining various aspects of diner history. There's also an interactive area called the Little Chef Diner, where kids can assemble pretend meals using plastic diner food and dishware.

The director and curator of the Culinary Arts Museum is Richard Gutman, one of the world's leading authori-ties on diners and diner history. His personal collection of diner memorabilia constitutes the bulk of what's on dis-play in the diners exhibit at the museum. By visiting and interacting with the exhibit, you're getting access to the best primary source material on American diners that you'll find anywhere.

It takes about an hour, maybe two, to fully absorb the entire exhibit, and it's well worth the time. If you like diners, this is a great starting point for developing a full appreciation of this unique and wonderful part of Ameri-can culinary history.

(*Note:* At press time the museum was undergoing a comprehensive inventory of its holdings. It will reopen to the public in the 2014–2015 academic year.)

The original Moody's Diner neon sign is on display.

The interior of the restored Every Ready Diner.

SONNY'S SCRAMBLED TOFU

SONNY'S BLUE BENN DINER, BENNINGTON, VT

The Blue Benn Diner is known far and wide for pioneering vegetarian diner cooking. They've got Vegetarian Chili, Vegetarian Lasagna, Veggie Meat Loaf, a Veggie Burrito, and a very flavorful Veggie Burger. Owner Sonny Monroe came up with this quick and easy tofu scramble for those seeking a tasty, meatless breakfast dish.

1	tablespoon olive oil
2	scallions, chopped
1	small green pepper, chopped
½	teaspoon curry powder
1	clove fresh garlic, chopped
1	pound silken tofu, drained and crumbled

In a skillet, heat the olive oil. Sauté the scallions, green pepper, and garlic in the heated oil until the green pepper is cooked. Add the tofu to the pan, mix in with the vegetables, and heat through. Plate and serve with homefries or toast. Serves 4.

STUFFED FRENCH TOAST

SEAPLANE DINER, PROVIDENCE, RI

In recent years, diner chefs have been doing some amazing things with French toast, topping and stuffing the egg-dipped slices of bread with all sorts of interesting, even exotic, ingredients. Try this cream cheese–stuffed version from Providence's Seaplane Diner. Or feel free to pull off I-95 just south of downtown Providence and try the real thing yourself at the actual diner. It's a classic.

- ½ teaspoon vanilla extract
- 2 eggs
- ½ teaspoon cinnamon
- 1 tablespoon brown sugar
-   Cream cheese
-   Strawberries
-   Blueberries
-   Banana
-   Whipped cream
-   Confectioners' sugar

1. To make the French toast batter, whisk the vanilla, eggs, cinnamon, and brown sugar together in a shallow bowl until well blended.

2. Butterfly the bread and add cream cheese inside each pocket (any amount is okay). Dip the bread into the French toast batter, then place the toast on the griddle or into a buttered skillet over medium heat. Cook for 2–3 minutes on each side until golden brown and the cream cheese is melted on the inside. Top with mixed fruit, whipped cream, and confectioners' sugar. Serves 2.

PLAIN DOUGHNUTS

MOODY'S DINER, WALDOBORO, ME

The bakers at Moody's arrive by 4:30 every morning, and the first thing they do is mix the doughnut batter and get the doughnuts cooking for the early morning crowd that will be expecting them hot out of the deep fryer.

You won't have to rise so early, however, if you want to make Moody's delectable doughnuts at home. It would behoove you to have a deep fryer of some sort or a high-sided skillet that can hold a decent amount of cooking oil to ensure the doughnuts come out crunchy and brown on the outside and tender and doughy within.

4	eggs
2	cups sugar
3	tablespoons (⅜ stick, 1½ ounces) margarine, melted
1	teaspoon vanilla extract
2	cups milk
5½	cups all-purpose flour, divided
4	teaspoons baking powder
3	teaspoons nutmeg
1¼	teaspoons salt

1. Beat the eggs with the sugar, margarine, and vanilla in a large mixing bowl. Mix in the milk, 3 cups of flour, and the remaining dry ingredients. Add the remaining flour until the dough is soft enough to handle. Let the dough rest in the bowl for 30 minutes.

2. Turn the bowl's contents onto a floured surface (a clean kitchen counter is fine) and roll out with a rolling pin. Cut circular sections of dough out with a doughnut cutter and fry in hot, 350°F oil until brown and crispy on the outside. Makes 32 doughnuts.

SMOKED SALMON EGGS BENEDICT

JIGGER'S HILL AND HARBOUR DINER, EAST GREENWICH, RI

Here's the perfect brunch dish for a special occasion. It has a variety of flavors and textures, from the poached eggs to the salmon filets to the rich hollandaise sauce to the sliced avocado on the side. The only tricky parts are poaching the eggs and whipping up the hollandaise. The rest is assembly work, and it makes for wonderfully tasty eating!

2	English muffins, sliced in half
	Cream cheese
¼	pound smoked salmon, sliced
4	eggs, poached
	Hollandaise sauce (see page 28)
1	ripe avocado, sliced

1. Toast the English muffins and spread them with cream cheese. Layer on the smoked salmon slices.

2. To poach the eggs, bring a shallow pan of water and a teaspoon of white vinegar (optional) almost to a boil. Crack each egg into a separate small bowl, then gently pour each cracked egg into the hot water. Cover the pan and simmer until the egg whites are cooked, about 4 minutes. Remove each poached egg from the water with a slotted spoon.

3. To assemble the eggs Benedict, place the poached eggs on top of the salmon slices, and ladle the hollandaise sauce over each serving. Place several avocado slices around each muffin. Serves 2.

A Rhode Island Charmer

✕ 145 Main Street
East Greenwich, RI 02818

☎ 401-884-6060

ⓘ www.hillandharbourdiner.com

Jigger's is one of many bright spots on Main Street in East Greenwich, Rhode Island.

The specials board at Jigger's.

Jigger's Hill and Harbourside Diner

There are few diners as charming and cozy as Jigger's Hill and Harbour in Rhode Island. Housed in an authentic 1950s Worcester diner car and lovingly refurbished just a couple of years ago, it's a diner that's not to be missed, both for its aesthetic qualities and for its fine-tasting, innovative food.

Though there has been an eatery in one form or another at this spot on Main Street in East Greenwich since 1915, the diner that's there today didn't arrive until 1950, when Worcester diner car number 826 was transported to the spot, and to great fanfare. The street was temporarily closed to traffic, and a band played as the diner was brought in on a large flatbed truck and placed on its new foundation. For the better part of four decades, a succession of owners served up food out of the Worcester car until 1983, when the diner fell on hard times and became a storage facility for an adjacent paint store.

In 1992, an enterprising woman named Carol Shriner purchased the building and began restoring the diner to its former glory. She brought the diner back to Main Street as a vibrant eatery for the next eight years, then she was followed by another woman named Iva, who kept the diner going until it was once again shuttered in 2011.

Steve and Karie Head bought the diner in 2012, and they have transformed the place into the gem that it is today. Their menu reflects the Heads' commitment to using fresh, locally grown and produced food as much as possible; many of their suppliers are nearby farmers and local businesses in Rhode Island and other parts of southern New England.

The quality of their ingredients and their culinary savoir faire shine through on virtually all their menu offerings. Standout dishes for breakfast include several eggs Benedict plates, each smothered in homemade hollandaise sauce. There's the Smoked Salmon Eggs Benedict (see page 43), which features the namesake fish filets along with cream cheese, poached eggs, capers, avocado slices, and hollandaise. More in the true diner vein is the Corned Beef Eggs Benedict, with a heaping helping of the diner's signature Black Angus Brisket Hash served on an English muffin with poached eggs and the ubiquitous hollandaise sauce.

From the griddle, there's an excellent Lemon Ricotta Stuffed French Toast with Blueberry Compote (see page 18). The Gingerbread Pancakes are also outstanding, and they come with

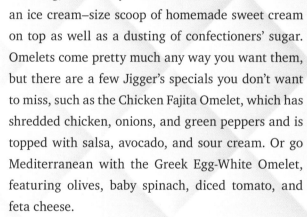
Jigger's famous gingerbread pancakes.

an ice cream–size scoop of homemade sweet cream on top as well as a dusting of confectioners' sugar. Omelets come pretty much any way you want them, but there are a few Jigger's specials you don't want to miss, such as the Chicken Fajita Omelet, which has shredded chicken, onions, and green peppers and is topped with salsa, avocado, and sour cream. Or go Mediterranean with the Greek Egg-White Omelet, featuring olives, baby spinach, diced tomato, and feta cheese.

Lunch is the only other meal served at Jigger's, which typically closes around 2:30 pm. Burgers, grilled panini sandwiches, and wraps are the main attractions, and the Heads pride themselves on using beef that comes only from farms that use no antibiotics or growth hormones on their livestock. They also make a wonderful apple walnut chicken salad that has found its way into a variety of sandwiches and that's also served straight up on a bed of romaine lettuce and garnished with craisins, croutons, and feta cheese. Jigger's makes its own potato chips, which come with a number of the sandwiches. You can also

order up a basket; they make a fine appetizer while waiting for your midday meal.

Jigger's also serves a specialty found virtually nowhere else except in Rhode Island: the Ice Cream Cabinet. Also known as a coffee cabinet, it's a milk shake–like beverage that's made with coffee ice cream, coffee syrup, and milk. Rhode Island's own Eclipse coffee syrup serves as the basis for these unusual concoctions, but at Jigger's they also do a chocolate version using Hershey's chocolate syrup. They also have vanilla and strawberry cabinets, each made with specially flavored Eclipse syrups. If all this sounds too exotic, you might instead want an ice cream float instead, which is made with Rhode Island's own Yacht Club soda, two scoops of vanilla ice cream, and a shot of Eclipse vanilla syrup to drive the vanilla point home.

Situated on one of the prettiest Main Streets in all of New England, Jigger's is a destination unto itself and well worth a visit to experience some diner haute cuisine and to sample a cabinet that's made of ice cream and syrup, not wood and brass.

Jigger's still retains many classic diner features.

WESTERN BAGEL SANDWICH

At the Seaplane Diner, they've transformed the classic Denver omelet into an easy-to-make sandwich—on a bagel, no less, which gives it a bit of an East Coast imprimatur. This is a very simple and quick one to make, and it satisfies first thing in the morning or as a midday meal.

3	eggs
½	cup ham, diced
½	cup onion, diced
½	cup green bell pepper, diced
	Cheese (optional), sliced or shredded
2	bagels, sliced, toasted, and buttered

1. Beat the eggs in a bowl. Add the diced ham, onions, and green peppers. Pour the egg mixture onto a heated grill or buttered skillet on medium-high heat.

2. Make an omelet or scramble the egg mixture, whichever you prefer. Add cheese during the cooking process, if desired. Place the eggs onto the bagel halves to make a sandwich. Serves 2.

PETE'S PARADISE PANCAKES

LAUREL DINER, SOUTHBURY, CT

These sweet, crunchy pancakes are named after Pete Homick, head cook and co-owner of the Laurel Diner, who invented this embellishment for pancakes, probably on a slow day when he had some time to play around on his famous hash-making griddle. You can use any recipe you wish to make pancakes for this dish; a recommended version is the from-scratch pancake recipe from Dottie's Diner earlier in this chapter (see Dottie's Homemade Buttermilk Pancakes, page 17).

1–2	tablespoons (⅛–¼ stick, ½–1 ounce) butter, divided
2–3	pancakes
½	cup pecans, chopped
¼	cup shredded sweetened coconut
1	banana, sliced into ¼-inch-thick rounds

Begin cooking the pancakes in a buttered pan or lightly buttered griddle. While the pancakes are cooking, place the sliced bananas on the griddle or on a second lightly buttered pan and grill lightly. When the bananas turn a light golden brown, remove them and place them on top of the cooked and plated pancakes. Top with the chopped pecans, coconut, and syrup. Serves 1.

Soups, Chowders, and Chilies

New England diners are famed for their interesting and unusual hashes, one-pot meals, seafood entrées—and their chowders. The varieties of chowders in the region—from the clear-broth style of Rhode Island to the creamy style in and around Boston to Maine's milky-brothed version—makes for some great variety in consistency, texture, and flavor. In addition to clam chowder recipes in this chapter, there are several variants in the form of seafood, haddock, scallop, and corn chowders, all guaranteed to satisfy any time of year.

Rounding out the offerings are a couple of chili recipes from such stalwarts as the Maine Diner and New Hampshire's Red Arrow Diner, a hearty Roasted Chicken and Vegetable Soup from Becky's in Portland, and a gourmet Butternut Squash Soup with Maple Crème Fraîche, Blue Cheese, and Cranberry from the Blue Plate Diner in Rhode Island.

But make no doubt about it: chowders take center stage here, as they're at the heart of New England cuisine. Explore and enjoy the variety in the recipes that follow. They represent an intriguing cross section of chowder ingredients and styles, and they all come from a wide variety of diners in New England. Vive la différence!

SEAFOOD CHOWDER

MAINE DINER, WELLS, ME

Perhaps the greatest legacy that co-owner Myles Henry left to this diner institution in Wells, Maine, is his recipe for seafood chowder. People have been known to drive hundreds of miles out of their way for a cup or bowl of this rich, flavorful bounty from the sea. With lots of fresh seafood and equal parts cream and milk, this chowder is firmly in the Maine tradition—not too thick, not too thin. One thing to keep in mind: the fresher the seafood you procure for it, the finer your Maine Diner seafood chowder will be.

1 whole 1-pound lobster (preferably from Maine, of course!)	2 cups milk
½ pound steaming clams	¼ cup parsley flakes
½ pound (26–30 count) raw shrimp	1 tablespoon paprika
½ pound sea scallops	2 medium potatoes, peeled and diced
1 10-ounce can baby clams	¼ pound salt pork, finely diced
½ cup (1 stick, 4 ounces) butter	1 medium onion, finely diced
2 cups light cream	Salt and pepper to taste
	Oyster crackers

1. In 1½ quarts water, boil lobster 15 minutes with a lid on the pot, being mindful not to let it boil over. Remove the lobster. In the same liquid, cook the steamers until they open. Remove the steamers. Again in the same liquid, cook the shrimp and scallops until done (not more than a couple of minutes). Leave these items in the pot with the broth and remove from heat.

2. Pick the lobster meat out of the shell, break it into bite-size pieces, and add it to the pot. Clean the tomalley (the lobster's liver, a greenish substance) out of the lobster cavity and add it to the pot—this serves as an excellent flavor booster. Add the baby clams (including juice), the butter, light cream, milk, parsley flakes, and paprika to the pot. Pick the steamed clams, removing the neck sheaths, and add the clams to the pot.

3. In another pot, boil the potatoes until just tender, then add to the pot.

4. In a frying pan, sauté the salt pork until brown and rendered. Add the onions and cook until tender. Add the contents of the frying pan to the pot.

5. Simmer the chowder on low heat until steaming hot. Add salt and pepper to taste. Serve with oyster crackers. Serves 4 hungry people.

BUTTERNUT SQUASH SOUP WITH MAPLE CRÈME FRAÎCHE, BLUE CHEESE, AND CRANBERRY

BLUE PLATE DINER, MIDDLETOWN, RI

Butternut squash is amazingly versatile. You can use it in appetizers, soups, main dishes, even desserts. This large, ochre-colored, bottom-heavy squash starts appearing in grocery stores (and on diner menus) in early autumn and sticks around until early winter. Here's a recipe for a hearty, flavorful, gourmet-style soup that uses the versatile butternut squash as its base.

SOUP

2	tablespoons (¼ stick, 1 ounce) butter
1	medium onion, chopped
2–3	pounds butternut squash, peeled, seeded, and cubed
6	cups low-sodium chicken stock
4	tablespoons brown sugar
½	cup crumbled blue cheese (preferably Maytag)
	Salt and freshly ground black pepper to taste
18	fresh whole cranberries

MAPLE CRÈME FRAÎCHE

¾	cup maple syrup (real is best)
¾	cup crème fraîche or sour cream

1. To make the soup, in a large stockpot, melt the butter and sauté the chopped onion. Cook until translucent, about 6–8 minutes over medium heat. Add the cubed butternut squash and cover with the chicken stock. Simmer for about 20 minutes or until the squash is tender to a fork's touch. Add the brown sugar and allow it to melt. Adjust seasoning to taste with salt and pepper.

2. Allow the mixture to cool slightly. Using a blender, puree the chunks of squash and some of the liquid and return it to the stockpot. Adjust the seasoning again to taste.

3. To make the maple crème fraîche, combine the syrup and crème fraîche in a bowl. Ladle the soup into bowls and top with blue cheese and a dollop of maple crème fraîche. Garnish with whole cranberries. Serves 6.

RHODE ISLAND CLAM CHOWDER

EVELYN'S DRIVE-IN, TIVERTON, RI

Most people think that clam chowder has by its very nature a thick, creamy broth that's laden with clams and potatoes, and by and large this is the case—in and around Boston, anyway.

The truth is, there are a variety of clam chowder types throughout New England—from the milky version found in Maine to various tomato-based chowders that pop up mostly in the southern New England states, when they appear at all.

Then there's the clear-broth, Rhode Island–style clam chowder that's prevalent throughout the Ocean State and many parts of Connecticut. At Evelyn's, a half diner/half clam shack on the peaceful shores of Nanaquaket Pond in eastern Rhode Island, Jane and Domenic Bitto serve up a wonderful version with a bit of a creamy twist.

1 gallon cold water	3 tablespoons clam base (preferably Better Than Bouillon)
2 cups raw clams, freshly chopped	1½ tablespoons freshly ground black pepper
1 medium onion, chopped	2 cups potatoes, diced into ½-inch cubes
1 cup (2 sticks, 8 ounces) butter	Salt and pepper to taste
4 bay leaves	Half-and-half (optional)

Place all the ingredients except the potatoes into a large soup pot. Bring to a boil over medium-high heat. Add the potatoes and cook until tender (approximately 10 minutes), using salt and pepper to taste. Ladle the chowder into bowls and serve with a splash of half-and-half, if desired. Serves 12–15.

61 Lowell Street
Manchester, NH 03101

☎ 603-626-1118

and

63 Union Square
Milford, NH 03055

☎ 603-249-9222

ⓘ www.redarrowdiner.com

Red Arrow Diner

There was a time when many diners were open 24 hours a day, 7 days a week. Such diners typically catered to factory workers and cops, who labored in shifts around the clock and who emerged ravenous and in search of a good, hot, affordable meal, no matter what time of day or night it happened to be.

That's how the Red Arrow Diner in Manchester, New Hampshire, got its start in 1922. Founded by David Lamontagne, the Red Arrow eventually grew to five locations in Manchester, back in the days when diners were the preferred place to go for a home-cooked meal and a hot cup of coffee.

Longtime Red Arrow employee Levi Letendre eventually bought the Red Arrow from Lamontagne and ran it well into the 1980s. With the rapid growth of fast food chains, the ancillary Red Arrow locations shut down, and the flagship Lowell Street Diner even closed its doors for a brief time in 1987 before being purchased by current owner, Carol Sheehan. Since taking over, Sheehan has aggressively shaped and marketed the Red Arrow into an institution of national renown.

The diner itself is in a surprisingly modest one-story, square-fronted, long and narrow brick building with a massive neon Red Arrow Diner sign suspended over the front door. Once you squeeze in through the skinny entrance, you find yourself staring down a long counter with customers perched on stools, reading the daily paper and bantering with the friendly waitstaff wedged between the counter and the kitchen. Off to the right of the front door are seven or eight tables by the front windows, the only other seating option at this popular diner. People line up along the wall behind the counter stools and wait patiently for a seat, and they'll all tell you that it's worth the wait.

This place has flourished under Sheehan's ownership for two main reasons: the great service that the staff provides and the food that the

Red Arrow serves up. No exotic fare here, just shoot-from-the-hip diner staples and specials served 'round the clock all year long. This is perhaps the only place where you can get breakfast, lunch, or dinner at any time of day or night, no questions asked. Want an omelet at 9 pm? No problem. How about meat loaf at 9 in the morning? Just ask.

As is the case with many diners, breakfast at the Red Arrow is the busiest time and most popular meal. There are countless variations on the eggs, meat, potatoes, and toast breakfasts, with everything from the Dinah-Mite Bursting Breakfast (four each of eggs, pancakes, sausage, *and* bacon, with home-fries and toast on the side) to the downright bashful two eggs with homefries, beans, grits, or hash browns.

You've been De-Virginized! The sticker given to all first-time Red Arrow diners.

Speaking of hash browns, this standard side dish may be what the Red Arrow Diner is best known for. They proudly serve their aptly named Famous Hash Brown Specials, where you get a plateful of golden hash browns and grilled onions mixed with ham, chili, kielbasa, or veggies; each plate is topped with a couple of slices of melted American cheese. One last thing to consider on the breakfast roster are the Eggs Benny—eggs Benedict dishes served with your choice of crab cakes, Canadian bacon, corned beef hash, or maple sausage patties; each delectable platter is topped with a generous ladling of home-made hollandaise sauce.

Lunch and dinner don't stray far from the diner standards, though keep in mind that the quality of food served at the Red Arrow is superior to that of many similar eateries. Adam Sandler is a native of Manchester and a regular customer at the diner, and they've named a burger after

A Red Arrow Diner hashbrown special.

him. The Red Arrow's chili is also renowned and is served by the cup or bowl (see page 56). Weekly dinner specials include Roast Port, Chicken Croquettes, Pot Roast, and Baked Stuffed Haddock.

It's hard to imagine who would frequent a place like the Red Arrow Diner in the middle of the night in a city the size of Manchester in this day and age. However, just show up at 2 or 3 am, and don't be surprised if there's a line snaking out the door. People are passionate about the Red Arrow, and as long as Pat Sheehan is at the helm, that's not going to change any time soon.

The Red Arrow's busy, convivial counter.

CHILI

This 24/7 diner in downtown Manchester, New Hampshire, serves chili round the clock, both by the cup or bowl and as an add-on to other dishes, such as hot dogs or omelets. This recipe calls for making a large batch, which is recommended, as it's a great dish for freezing or refrigerating and having more later on.

4	tablespoons (½ stick, 2 ounces) butter, melted
½	cup green bell pepper, diced
½	cup yellow or white onion, diced
2½	pounds ground beef
¼	cup chili powder
½	tablespoon cayenne pepper
½	tablespoon cumin
½	tablespoon crushed red pepper flakes
2	12-ounce cans chili sauce
1	15-ounce can red kidney beans, with sauce
1	28-ounce can diced tomatoes

In a large pot, sauté the peppers and onions in the melted butter over medium heat for 2–3 minutes. Add the ground beef and spices and continue to stir and cook until the hamburger is almost cooked through. Add the chili sauce, kidney beans, and diced tomatoes, and blend thoroughly. Reduce heat and simmer for 30 minutes. Serves 8–10.

SCALLOP CHOWDER

BETSY'S DINER, FALMOUTH, MA

Betsy's is a godsend on Cape Cod, perhaps the only true stainless steel and glass diner in the region that's still doing it right—great food, friendly service, and a neighborhood feel. Here's the diner's recipe for a very nice chowder that calls for sweet, tender bay scallops.

8 slices thick-cut bacon	6 red potatoes, cut into ½-inch cubes
1 onion, chopped	½ cup whipping cream
¾ teaspoons fresh or dried thyme	2 tablespoons (¼ stick, 1 ounce) butter, divided
4 cups bottled clam juice	1 pound bay scallops
½ cup dry white wine	Salt and pepper to taste

1. Cook the bacon in a sauté pan until crisp, and transfer cooked bacon to paper towels. When cooled, chop the bacon into small pieces. Set aside.

2. Drain all but 2 tablespoons of bacon fat from the pan. Add the onion and thyme to the pan and sauté over low heat until the onions are light golden, about 10 minutes.

3. In a medium-size pot, add the clam juice, white wine, and potatoes. Bring to a boil. Reduce the heat and simmer until the potatoes are tender, about 15–20 minutes. Add the cooked onions and thyme to the pot and simmer. Then add the cream and bacon, stirring regularly, and continue to simmer.

4. Melt 1 tablespoon of butter in the sauté pan, add half the scallops, and sauté until golden brown. Set aside. Repeat with the remainder of the butter and scallops. Add all the cooked scallops to the pot and stir, with salt and pepper to taste. Serves 5–6.

DICK'S CORN CHOWDER

MAINE DINER, WELLS, ME

Myles Henry's world-famous Seafood Chowder (see page 50) isn't the only great chowder on the menu at the Maine Diner. Brother Dick's Corn Chowder, though not as well known, is every bit as good, with legions of locals (and those rare non-seafood lovers) opting for this not-quite-vegetarian version. If you're in a chowder mood at the Maine, try ordering a cup of each and do your own side-by-side taste test. Chances are you'll have a hard time deciding which one is best.

2–3	large peeled potatoes, cut into pieces	3	15-ounce cans creamed corn
½	pound bacon	½	gallon milk
1	onion, diced	1	15-ounce can whole kernel sweet corn
1	pint light cream	1	cup (2 sticks, 8 ounces) butter

1. Parboil the potatoes. Fry the bacon in a pan, then remove, crumble, and set aside. Leave a small amount of grease in the pan. Add the onion to the grease and sauté over medium-low heat. Slowly add the cream to the pan, then add some of the creamed corn, stirring regularly.

2. In a separate pot, warm the milk and add the potatoes, butter, the remaining creamed corn, and the whole kernel sweet corn. Divide the crumbled bacon between the pan and the pot. Add the pan mixture to the warmed pot mixture, with salt and pepper to taste. Serves 8–12.

ROASTED CHICKEN AND VEGETABLE SOUP

BECKY'S DINER, PORTLAND, ME

This is chicken vegetable soup made the old-fashioned way—from scratch. It's pretty labor intensive, but the ends (killer soup) justify the means (*lots* of cooking and chopping). This is a meal in a pot that's perfect for a winter's day or as an antidote to help clear up a head cold.

2	whole bone-in chicken breasts	4	tablespoons (½ stick, 2 ounces) butter, divided
2	whole sweet potatoes, pricked with a fork	1	onion, diced
1	head fresh garlic	½	red bell pepper, diced
2	carrots, peeled and chopped (reserve trimmings)	1	portobello mushroom, diced
3	stalks celery, chopped (reserve trimmings)	1	zucchini, diced
3	quarts water	1	summer squash, diced
	Several sprigs fresh thyme, divided		Salt and pepper to taste

1. Preheat the oven to 350°F. Roast the chicken on a rack in the oven with the sweet potatoes and garlic head in a lightly greased roasting pan for 1½ hours. Remove and let cool. Pick the meat off the bones and season with salt, pepper, and half of the thyme. Save the bones for the chicken stock. Set the roasted sweet potatoes and garlic head aside.

2. In a large pot, boil the chicken bones, carrots, celery, and reserved vegetable trimmings in water for 45 minutes.

3. In a pan, sauté the onions with butter under medium heat for 5 minutes. Add the peppers and mushrooms and set aside. In a second pan, sauté the zucchini and squash in butter. Season with salt, pepper, and thyme, and set aside.

4. Drain the stock and remove and discard the bones. Add the roasted sweet potatoes and garlic to the stock and puree till smooth. Then add the cooked vegetables, chicken, and remaining thyme. Serves 4.

"Eat Heavy"

Betsy's is a welcome sight for diner lovers visiting Cape Cod.

Betsy's Diner

"Eat Heavy" is the battle cry at Betsy's, according to co-owners Dave and Karen Chandler, who have owned and run Betsy's Diner for nearly 20 years. Dave says he co-opted the phrase from a diner he once visited in New Jersey, and you'll see the slogan on the walls and the menus and in neon on the front of the building as you enter.

Betsy's is set back in a small parking lot on Main Street in the picturesque Cape Cod town of Falmouth, Massachusetts. It's a bit of an anachronism, given that much of the rest of the town is done up in the quaint colonial New England clapboard style found throughout the Cape. Dave has had more than his fair share of dustups with the local zoning commission, but Betsy's has been grandfathered in on many of its physical features, and it's a beloved place locally.

Diner aficionados will appreciate the original stainless steel and glass exterior and curved-ceiling interior of this classic 1957 Mountain View diner, which started its life as the Peter Pan Diner in Kuhnsville, Pennsylvania. The structure was moved to its current site in 1992, and the Chandlers became owners two years later. The diner's two rooms can seat nearly 120 patrons, and this place can get crazy busy, especially during the summer months.

Dave's path to diner ownership was long and complicated. He had no intention of purchasing a diner, or any restaurant for that matter, until he laid eyes on Betsy's in the early 1990s, at a time when he was looking for a business to own. Wife Karen wasn't so sure about buying the diner when Dave initially suggested it, but once the decision was made, she has been along as Dave's invaluable partner in the business ever since.

Initially the Chandlers stuck closely to the menu they inherited from Betsy's previous owners. Dave added some Italian dishes, but to this day the offerings still cling closely to classic American diner food.

In keeping with the "Eat Heavy" theme, there's a big plate of liver and onions; a knockwurst, sauerkraut, baked beans, and coleslaw platter; chicken, ziti, and broccoli in cream sauce; and a hot, open-faced turkey sandwich with stuffing, mashed potatoes, cranberry sauce, and gravy, among other high-calorie offerings.

Burgers are very popular here, and they come in the half-pound variety with all the usual trimmings, plus blue cheese, ham (yes, ham), and chili as other options. You may have as many or as few toppings as you wish. There's also some excellent fried chicken from a recipe that Albert (one of Dave's chefs) insisted was better that what the diner had been serving for years. Dave gave it a try with the customers, and thus Albert's Fried Chicken was born, which has found a permanent place on the menu.

Given its proximity to the ocean, seafood plays a big role in the lunch and dinner offerings. Fried clams come in the whole belly and strip varieties and can be served either on a roll with French fries on the side, or as part of a platter with fries and coleslaw. Good old-fashioned fish cakes (a slowly vanishing New England specialty) are served with baked beans, as are Betsy's crab cakes. On the lighter side, there's a very tasty broiled scrod topped with bread crumbs and a grilled swordfish steak, good choices for those who crave seafood but wish to avoid the deep fryer. The clam chowder is also excellent. (Go with the bowl size—it's only a dollar more—and share it with your dining companions.)

There's a constantly rotating roster of specials, many of which are standard items on the menu that have been discounted that day. Additionally, there are such exotic items as Baked Ham, Asparagus, and Swiss Cheese Casserole; a baked stuffed chicken dinner; a pot roast dinner; and a generously portioned lobster salad roll plate that comes with the lobster on a grilled brioche bun and a big piece of watermelon on the side. Dave likes to feature what he calls a Workman's Special several times a week that consists of a sandwich or platter at a very affordable price.

Breakfast is pretty straightforward and perhaps most distinguished by the massive portions served up throughout the day. The Filled Pancakes (lots of options) are particularly massive, and the omelets are of the three-egg variety.

Betsy's is a family place, and at any time of day or evening, you'll find lots of little kids in attendance, many of them ordering from the very affordable Little Diner's menu. Some of the younger waitstaff first came to Betsy's in baby carriages a couple of decades ago and are now part of Betsy's team. Dave and Karen like the family atmosphere, and as such, no alcohol is sold or served at the diner.

The Chandlers, who live literally a stone's throw from the diner, are hands-on owners, which is always a sign of a well-run place, where you can expect good service, great food, and a friendly, relaxed atmosphere. Betsy's should be the first place you stop before heading further out on the Cape in search of fun in the sun.

QUAHOG CHOWDER

This chowder is known far and wide (as far and wide as you can go) in southwestern Rhode Island. Recipe creator and Wickford Diner owner Stu Tucker is a very busy man, owning a few restaurants in the Wickford area and running a restaurant supply business out of an old warehouse in North Kingstown. This chowder is probably the most popular item at his diner and his other restaurants as well, and with good reason.

Tucker's Quahog Chowder packs a punch of real clam flavor that sometimes goes missing or gets lost in other chowders. He says there are two important rules to follow when making up a batch: get fresh or frozen chopped quahog clams, as opposed to the many other clam varieties that are often used in chowders, and shut off the heat on the cooking pot as soon as the full chowder begins to boil. Tucker is a firm believer that any extra cooking takes the flavor out of the chowder, so bring it to a boil, shut it off, let it sit, and serve it up!

⅛–¼	pound salt pork, ground or finely diced	3	pounds potatoes, diced into ½-inch cubes
¾	pound onions, diced	1	tablespoon Worcestershire sauce
1	quart water *or*	3	cups fresh or frozen quahog clams, chopped
3	cups quahog or clam juice *or*		Salt and pepper to taste
	Quahog concentrate or clam base		

1. Render the salt pork in a large, heavy cooking pot (the heavier the cooking pot, the better). Sauté the onions in the rendered salt pork. Add the water or the quahog/clam juice and cook over medium heat until steaming. Add the potatoes and cook or simmer until the potatoes are soft. Add the Worcestershire sauce and salt and pepper to taste.

2. Fold in the chopped quahog clams, turn up the heat, and bring to a boil, then shut off the burners immediately and let the chowder sit for a few minutes before serving. Serves 8–10.

ATLANTIC HADDOCK CHOWDAH

BECKY'S DINER, PORTLAND, ME

With Becky's location hard by the Portland commercial fishing harbor, the fish and other seafood served here is as fresh as it can be. (Many of the local fishermen are regulars.) The diner's Haddock Chowdah is one of its most popular dishes, either as an opener or as a meal unto itself.

1 medium onion, chopped	1 cup water (to cook potatoes)
4 tablespoons (½ stick, 2 ounces) margarine or butter	1 pound skinless haddock fillets (cod or hake may be substituted)
1 teaspoon black pepper	½ cup whole milk
½ teaspoon salt	1 5-ounce can evaporated milk (not skim)
½ teaspoon garlic powder	3 slices bacon, cooked and crumbled
1 pound boiling potatoes, peeled and diced	Salt and pepper to taste

1. In a large, heavy pot, cook the chopped onion in the margarine or butter over medium-low heat, stirring until the onion is softened. Add the pepper, salt, garlic powder, potatoes, and just enough water to cover the potatoes. Boil until the potatoes are tender, about 8–10 minutes.

2. Lay the fish fillets on top of the potatoes. Don't add or drain off any water at this point. Cover and simmer until the fillets begin to flake apart, about 5–8 minutes. Add the milk and evaporated milk to reach your desired consistency. Turn up the heat, but don't bring to a boil. Add the bacon, seasoning with additional salt and pepper to taste. Serves 4–6.

Good Things Do Come in Small Packages

🍴 64 Brown Street
North Kingstown, RI 02852

☎ 401-295-5477

ⓘ www.quahog.com/diner.html

Wickford Diner

In the tiny, charming harborside hamlet of Wickford, Rhode Island, you'll find the equally diminutive and adorable Wickford Diner, an eatery that's been on the Wickford waterfront in one form or another for at least 75 years.

Owner Stu Tucker is a locally known restaurateur and restaurant supplies dealer. His office is squirreled away in the dark interior of his dilapidated North Kingstown warehouse, which is stacked floor to ceiling with every type of used restaurant appliance and gizmo imaginable. He's a walking encyclopedia of local restaurant history, and this may be why he took an interest in the Wickford Diner a number of years ago and refurbished it into the charming spot it is today.

The Wickford is built around an old Tierney diner that Tucker renovated and added on to by purchasing the building next door and outfitting it with extra seating in a more traditional restaurant style. Where you want to be for your diner fix, however, is in the diner portion, with its curved roof and its lunch counter with 10 barstools.

Seafood is what's cooking at the Wickford, and the place is best known for Stu's Quahog Chowder (see page 62), a thick, rich, flavorful chowder that captures all the freshness of the local waters. The chowder is served in white and red varieties, and there's also a very tasty lobster bisque that's made every day.

A nice complement to the chowder (or to anything on the menu, for that matter) is the stuffed Quahog clams, also known as "stuffies." These clamshell halves are loaded with minced Quahog clams mixed in with a spicy stuffing and baked in the oven before they're served up. The lobster roll is also very popular, as are the clam cakes, another bite-size treat that's great for dunking into a bowl of chowder.

If you happen to be at the Wickford during breakfast hours, try the massive Breakfast Burrito or the Grilled Portuguese Muffin, perhaps

the most famous and popular item on the morning menu. The French toast, pancakes, and omelets are also outstanding. Next door, Tucker has a food emporium, where you may purchase cooked seafood items or pick up a bag of frozen Quahog clams to make his famous chowder at home yourself. It's well worth a stop at this diner in this cozy little seaside town, which is one of the Ocean State's better kept secrets.

CHILI

MAINE DINER, WELLS, ME

This is a rather mild version of chili by today's standards, but feel free to make it spicier by upping the amount of chili powder, crushed red pepper flakes, and Tabasco sauce you put in. (Keep in mind that the horseradish will add a bit of New England–style kick to the chili, so don't overdo it with the other spices.)

1	pound ground chuck	2	cups water
1	small onion, coarsely chopped	½	teaspoon salt
1	clove fresh garlic, finely chopped	½	teaspoon pepper
1	tomato, diced	1	tablespoon thyme
1	15-ounce can chili con carne	1	teaspoon chili powder
1	15-ounce can red kidney beans, drained	½	teaspoon crushed red pepper flakes
⅓	cup horseradish		Dash of Tabasco sauce

Sauté the ground chuck in a heavy pot, then drain off the grease. Add the onion and garlic and cook over medium heat for 1–2 minutes, until the flavors combine. Add the remaining ingredients and cook uncovered over low heat for approximately 3 hours. Serves 4–6.

FISH CHOWDER

MOODY'S DINER, WALDOBORO, ME

This is a very nice, simple, flavorful fish chowder, done in the Maine style, with a milky broth rather than a creamy one. As is the case with all seafood chowders, the fresher the fish, the tastier the dish.

4	tablespoons (½ stick, 2 ounces) butter, divided
⅔	cup onions, diced
3	cups potatoes, diced
2	pounds haddock or similar fish filet
2	cups milk
1	5-ounce can evaporated milk
	Salt and pepper to taste

1. Melt half the butter in a heavy pot over medium heat. Sauté the onions until tender. Add the potatoes, cover with water, and place fish on top of the potatoes. Cover the pot and simmer for 20 minutes.

2. In the meantime, heat the milk in a small pan until it's scalding. Stir the milk into the pot and add the remaining butter. Season with salt and pepper to taste, and let stand 30 minutes for flavors to come together. Serves 6.

Diner Classics

There are certain dishes that are synonymous with diners—meat loaf, open-faced roast turkey sandwiches, mac and cheese, chicken pot pie—all hearty, stick-to-your-ribs meals that are as filling as they are affordable.

This chapter contains several recipes for meat loaf, and though they all have the same basic ingredients and cooking methods, there are subtle differences worth noting, especially in the seasonings. Peruse each one and decide which one appeals most to your tastes, then give it a try. Some people who say they hate meat loaf change their minds when they're served a variation on the recipe. Have fun with these and see if there's any one in particular that's a crowd pleaser in your home.

Hearty one-pot meals like beef stew and New England boiled dinner are geared toward feeding a crowd, but they also make for great leftovers—especially the boiled dinner, which provides the basis for red flannel hash. These dishes are best when prepared on the stovetop and not in the slow cooker, where all the flavor tends to get cooked right out of them.

There are also a few different recipes for the diner classic chicken pot pie. Again, they're close in their general characteristics, but their differences make each one shine in their own unique way, even if it's something as simple as the Agawam Diner's insistence on serving the pie by flipping it over and pouring more gravy over the bottom/top.

Have fun with all these variations, and be sure to swing by some of these diners and try the real thing. Who knows, maybe your version will outshine theirs, in which case you may consider opening your own diner!

DOTTIE'S MEAT LOAF

DOTTIE'S DINER, WOODBURY, CT

Dottie's meat loaf stands out from the crowded field of diner meat loafs by virtue of the finely diced red and green bell peppers mixed into the loaf and the use of marjoram and Dijon mustard as the main flavor enhancers. It's also served with a rich, dark, homemade beef gravy that goes great on top of the meat loaf once it's sliced and served.

MEAT LOAF

- ¼ cup red bell pepper, finely diced
- ¼ cup green bell pepper, finely diced
- ¼ cup white or yellow onion, diced
- 1½ pounds ground beef
- 2 tablespoons Dijon mustard
- 2 eggs, beaten lightly
- ¾ cup bread crumbs
- 1 tablespoon marjoram

GRAVY

- 2 tablespoons red peppers, chopped
- 2 tablespoons green peppers, chopped
- ¼ cup onion, chopped
- 1 teaspoon jalapeño pepper, chopped
- 4 tablespoons (½ stick, 2 ounces) butter
- ¼ cup all-purpose flour
- 3 cups water (add beef base or bullion to taste)

1. To make the meat loaf, preheat the oven to 400°F. Mix all the ingredients together in a large bowl. Fold the loaf into a greased 5 x 9-inch bread pan. Bake for 1 hour.

2. To make the gravy, sauté the peppers and onions in the butter. Slowly add the flour and water, and cook over low heat until brown and thickened to the desired consistency. Cut the meat loaf into individual slices and top with gravy. Serves 6.

MEAT LOAF DINNER

SEAPLANE DINER, PROVIDENCE, RI

The Seaplane's version of meat loaf is simple and straightforward. That's one of the things that makes it so good. Serve it with fresh mashed potatoes and your favorite boiled or steamed vegetables, and you've got a blue plate special dinner that's satisfying any time of year. The proportions here are quite large—can anyone say "meat loaf sandwich"? Have one loaf for dinner and the other between pieces of bread later in the week.

3   pounds ground beef

4   eggs

1   cup ketchup

½   cup Italian-style bread crumbs

1   teaspoon granulated onion powder

1   teaspoon granulated garlic powder

½   cup fresh parsley, chopped

    Black pepper to taste

Preheat the oven to 350°F. Combine all the ingredients in a large mixing bowl and mix together thoroughly. Grease two 5 x 9-inch bread pans, and place equal amounts of the loaf mixtures into each. Bake for 1 hour and 15 minutes until the meat is thoroughly browned inside. Serves 8–10.

BECKY'S CHICKEN POT PIE

BECKY'S DINER, PORTLAND, MAINE

Perhaps the most famous dish at Becky's Diner is the Roast Turkey, which is served every day they're open, year-round. It was featured on *Diners, Drive-Ins and Dives* several years ago, and it has triggered thousands of orders from customers at Becky's since then.

Making the roast turkey at home is a major production, but a close relative (that's easier to make) is her equally famous and tasty Chicken Pot Pie. If you have a hankering for some comfort food with lots of healthy ingredients, Becky's Chicken Pot Pie will do very nicely.

2 whole bone-in chicken breasts	Several peppercorns
4 carrots, peeled and chopped (reserve trimmings)	1 onion, chopped (reserve trimmings)
1 bunch celery, chopped (reserve trimmings)	4 tablespoons (½ stick, 2 ounces) butter
2–3 cups chicken broth	¼ cup all-purpose flour
¼ cup vinegar	½ cup frozen peas
1 bay leaf	2 9-inch refrigerated piecrusts
	Salt and pepper to taste

1. Preheat the oven to 350°F. Roast the chicken breasts in the oven for 60 minutes in a shallow roasting pan. Remove and let cool. Pick the meat off the bones, then add salt and pepper to taste.

2. In a medium-size pot, boil the carrots and celery in 3 quarts of water for 45 minutes. Drain the cooked vegetables and set aside.

3. In a large pot, heat the chicken broth with the reserved vegetable trimmings, vinegar, bay leaf, and peppercorns.

4. In a pan, sauté the onions in butter over medium-low heat for approximately 10 minutes. Add the flour, season with salt and pepper, and simmer for 10 minutes, whisking occasionally to make a roux. Add the onion roux to the hot chicken broth. Then add the chicken, boiled carrots and celery, and peas, mix thoroughly, and reduce over medium heat to a gravy-like consistency.

5. Before assembling the pie, preheat the oven to 375°F. Lightly moisten the rim of one pie shell. Pour the filling into the shell and drape the other pastry over the filling, pressing the top and bottom pastries together along the edge. Trim the pastry flush with the edge of the pan. Using the back of a fork, press the tines along the edge to seal the pastry. Bake for 50 minutes. Serves 2–4.

TURKEY CROQUETTES

CHELSEA ROYAL DINER, WEST BRATTLEBORO, VT

Turkey Croquettes appear as a special on Tuesday nights at the Chelsea Royal Diner. This recipe calls for some baking and some frying, so roll up your sleeves and prepare to go to work. It's a great one to use when you've got Thanksgiving leftovers and you want something more interesting and flavorful than just a plate of leftover turkey and trimmings.

CROQUETTES

1	cup celery, minced
½	cup onions, minced
4	tablespoons (½ stick, 2 ounces) butter
1½–2	pounds leftover turkey, finely chopped/minced (ground turkey may be substituted)
¼	cup all-purpose flour
	Fresh parsley, chopped
4	cups milk
	Salt and pepper to taste

FOR BREADING AND FRYING

2	cups all-purpose flour
3	eggs, whipped with a little water
4	cups seasoned bread crumbs
2–3	cups vegetable oil

1. To make the croquettes, preheat the oven to 325°F. In a large pot, melt the butter and cook the celery and onion over low heat until they're translucent. Add the turkey, flour, parsley, and salt and pepper to taste and mix well, forming a paste-like consistency.

2. Add the milk slowly, stirring constantly until you have an oatmeal-like texture. Spread and press the mixture evenly onto a buttered cookie sheet. Cover with parchment paper, pressing it lightly onto the croquette mixture. Bake for 40–45 minutes. Remove the cookie sheet from the oven, set it aside to cool, then scoop the croquette mixture into balls with a small ice cream scoop.

3. To make the breading, cover the croquette balls with flour, dip them into the egg mixture, and roll each one in the seasoned bread crumbs. Panfry the breaded croquettes in a cast-iron skillet (or other thick-bottom pan) in about ½ inch of vegetable oil, turning them until golden brown all around. Makes 6–8 croquettes.

(In keeping with the Thanksgiving theme, these croquettes go great with cranberry sauce, mashed potatoes, and fresh steamed vegetables.)

Dottie's Diner for Doughnuts and More

🍴 740 South Main Street
Woodbury, Connecticut 06798

☎ 203-263-2516

and

Dottie's 2

🍴 146 Grand Street
Waterbury, CT 06702

☎ 475-235-2482

🌐 www.dottiesdiner.com

Dottie's is tucked away in a tiny strip mall in Woodbury, Connecticut.

Dottie's Diner

Dottie's Diner, in the antiques-store mecca of Woodbury, Connecticut, has had two lives, both of them distinctive and successful. For decades prior to 2006, the Phillips family ran the place and served up some very fine diner food, including a locally famous chicken pot pie and doughnuts that were made fresh on the premises every morning. When the Phillipses decided to sell and get out of the restaurant business, a collective hush fell over the town as loyal patrons waited to see what would happen next. Enter Dorothy (Dorie) Sperry, who bought the business and forged ahead with all the warm, comforting food that people had been used to getting at Dottie's over the years.

Initially, Dorie stuck close to the Phillips's menu, much to the delight of the locals. Over time, she has added her own special dishes and touches, and her changes have been more than warmly received. Some are subtle, such as her offering the Chicken Pot Pie in its chicken-only original form and an alternate version augmented with fresh vegetables (see page 86). Others are more upscale, such as the pan-seared sea bass and the vegetable risotto. A 35-year veteran of the food service business, Dorie's last gig before buying the diner was as a manager of the five-star, five-diamond Mayflower Inn in nearby Washington Depot, long considered one of the nation's finest restaurants. (A couple of the cooks at Dottie's came from the Mayflower.)

Dorie also redecorated Dottie's from the floor up, lightening and brightening it up with aqua- and cream-colored Naugahyde booths, off-white walls, and recessed lighting just beneath the ceiling line around the entire dining room. She also replaced the original counter with a new one, albeit in the same serpentine configuration as its predecessor. This made the regular counter crowd feel comfortable with the changes, and to this day there's always lots of friendly chatter, often between total strangers perched on the counter's numerous stools. The waitstaff is super friendly and experienced, adding to the overall bonhomie of the place.

Dottie's is synonymous with doughnuts. The Phillips family started the tradition years ago, cooking up fresh batches every morning and stocking the pastry cases behind the counter and beside the cash register. Michael Stern of Roadfood.com has called them the best doughnuts anywhere in America—high praise indeed. Be sure to arrive early to make sure you snag one to have with your morning coffee, or score a bagful at the cash register to take home or on the road. Another outstanding breakfast treat is Dorie's homemade Coffee Cake (see page 34), with a sweet and crunchy topping on the dense, flavorful cake. It's cut into brownie-like squares and is also on display by the register.

Midday and evening favorites start with the aforementioned chicken pot pie. Another Phillips original, the pie's crust is light and flaky, the chicken tender and flavorful, the gravy rich and creamy, and the cooked vegetables within (should you choose Dorie's version) are light and refreshing. Each pot pie is petite (about 6 inches in diameter) and comes with a heaping helping of home-made mashed potatoes and fresh steamed vegetables on the side.

The homemade Meat Loaf is another suppertime standout (see page 70). Dottie's version of this diner classic is spiced up with some finely chopped bell peppers, a couple of spoonfuls of Dijon mustard, and in the gravy, some diced jalapeño pepper. It, too, comes with mashed potatoes and steamed fresh vegetables. On the lighter side are some very nice full-meal-size salads—a Cobb, a Caesar, and more. Home-baked pies and a thick, rich bread pudding are top choices for those who still have room for dessert. Another vestige of the Phillips era is Dottie's amazing Lemon Meringue Pie.

This little gem in western Connecticut is tucked away in a tidy strip mall with black awnings and a classic clapboard New England façade. The only way you'll know you're in the right place is by the pastel-painted wooden DOTTY'S DINER sign nailed to the roof. So, keep your eyes peeled and your appetite sharpened because you're in for a treat when you pull into Dottie's.

Dottie's serpentine counter and 1950s retro décor are popular with the diner's patrons.

BECKY'S BEEF STEW

BECKY'S DINER, PORTLAND, ME

This version of beef stew is a little more complicated (and a lot more tasty) than most other beef stew recipes. The garlic, red wine, roux, and thyme boost the flavor and texture to a higher level than your run-of-the-mill beef stew, elevating what is often a bland, chewy experience into a deep, rich, flavorful meat-and-potatoes meal.

4	carrots, peeled (reserve peels)
½	turnip, peeled (reserve peels)
3	Maine russet potatoes, peeled and chopped
2	pounds stew beef
1	cup Syrah (or red table wine)
1	bay leaf
2	cloves fresh garlic
	Several sprigs fresh thyme
	Salt and pepper to taste

BEEF STOCK

2	cups water
	Beef bones
1	bay leaf
¼	cup vinegar
	Several peppercorns to taste

ROUX

1	large onion, peeled and chopped
½	stick butter
½	cup all-purpose flour

1. Preheat the oven to 325°F. In a large pot, boil the carrots and turnip for 45 minutes. Add the potatoes after 25 minutes.

2. In another large pot, add the beef and season with salt and pepper. Then add the red wine, bay leaf, garlic, and thyme. Sear the beef over medium-high heat until browned. Separate the beef from the wine, retaining the liquid for the sauce.

3. To make the beef stock, in a medium-size saucepan, combine all ingredients, adding the reserved carrot and turnip peels. Bring to a boil, then reduce the heat and simmer for approximately 30 minutes until the stock begins to thicken. Remove and discard the beef bones.

4. To make the roux, sauté the onion in a large, clean pan. Add butter and flour and stir constantly under medium-high heat.

5. Combine the leftover wine from the beef marinade and the beef stock with the onion/roux mixture. Once thickened, add the boiled vegetables and beef. Roast in a covered pot in the oven for 2½ hours. Serves 6.

ROAST TURKEY WITH SAUSAGE STUFFING

BLUE PLATE DINER, MIDDLETOWN, RI

Whether it's for the holidays or just an old-fashioned dinnertime feast any time of year, roast turkey is a staple on diner menus throughout New England. It may be served as an open-faced sandwich over sliced bread and smothered in gravy with mashed potatoes and boiled/steamed veggies on the side; or it may appear as a straight-up Thanksgiving-style turkey dinner with all the trimmings. Here's a wonderful version from the Blue Plate Diner that is accompanied by a fairly basic yet highly delectable sausage stuffing.

STUFFING

- ½ cup (1 stick, 4 ounces) butter
- 2 stalks celery, diced
- ¼ Spanish onion, diced
- ½ pound uncooked sausage meat (any sausage meat works)
- 2 cups chicken stock
- 1 loaf stale white bread, cubed
- Salt and pepper to taste

TURKEY

- 1 18-pound turkey (preferably fresh)
- ½ cup (1 stick, 4 ounces) unsalted butter, softened
- 1 quart chicken stock (turkey stock is better, if you can get it)
- Salt and pepper to taste

1. To make the stuffing, preheat the oven to 350°F. In sauté pan, heat the butter and add the celery and onion. Cook for 4–6 minutes until limp and translucent. Add the sausage and cook until fragrant, an additional 6 minutes over low heat.

2. In a separate bowl, combine the chicken stock and white bread. Add the sausage mixture. Season with salt and pepper to taste. Makes 8 cups.

3. Set aside enough stuffing (approximately 4 cups) to fill the turkey. Place extra stuffing in a greased baking pan and bake, covered, for approximately 30 minutes.

4. To prepare the turkey, preheat the oven to 325°F. Place the oven rack in the lowest position.

5. Remove the turkey neck and giblets, thoroughly rinse the turkey, and pat the skin dry so it will crisp up during roasting.

6. Put the turkey breast-side up on a rack in a roasting pan and fill the body cavity with stuffing. Rub the skin with the softened butter and season liberally with salt and pepper. Cover with aluminum foil.

7. Place the turkey in a roasting pan with 2 cups of stock in the bottom. Baste the bird every 30 minutes with juices from the bottom of the pan. Add stock to the drippings as needed to counterbalance evaporation.

8. Remove aluminum foil after 2½ hours. Roast the turkey until the thermometer in the middle of a thigh is 170°F (after 4 hours, approximately). Remove from the oven and let rest for 15–20 minutes or until the internal temperature reaches 180°F. Slice and serve with extra stuffing. Serves 12.

Tumble In and Stay a While

✕ 1 Main Street
    Claremont, NH 03743

☎ 603-504-6561

One of the diner's patrons built this 3-foot-long wooden scale model of the diner.

Much of the Tumble Inn's colorful tile and glass work has been lovingly restored.

Daddypop's Tumble Inn Diner

One of the brighter spots on the quiet streets of downtown Claremont in western New Hampshire is Daddypop's Tumble Inn Diner, a mainstay business that has hung in there for decades to become a diner legend of sorts in New England. In the capable hands of the Smith family for the past 15 years, the diner has stabilized from its somewhat rocky past and built a steady clientele of loyal breakfast and lunch customers.

Back in the mid-twentieth century, when the factories and mills of Claremont were humming with round-the-clock activity, the Tumble Inn Diner was the place to go for a meal and a hot cup of coffee. As the workplaces began shutting down and moving away, the diner's fortunes became uncertain, and a succession of owners tried their hand at running the place from the late 1980s to the mid-1990s.

During that time, New Hampshire native Ken Smith had left the Granite State and settled near York, Pennsylvania, where he became the owner of Daddypop's Diner, which he still owns today. On one of his many trips back to the land of his youth, Smith heard the Tumble Inn was up for sale, so he checked it out. He bought the dining car building in 1997, fixed it up, and turned the day-to-day management of the establishment over to his daughter Deborah. To establish the Pennsylvania–New Hampshire connection, he added "Daddypop's" to the front end of the Tumble Inn Diner name, and a two-state, two-diner chain of sorts was established.

Perhaps the best thing about Daddypop's Tumble Inn is the magnificent 1941 Worcester dining car that houses the vintage booths, stools, and service counter of the eatery. It's been lovingly restored to its near-original look. Outside, Tumble Inn Diner is boldly spelled out in red letters on a white background beneath the diner's front-facing windows. Inside, the tile work on the floor and counters is in great shape, as are the half-dozen or so wooden booths, wood trim, and tile backsplash

Daddypop's Tumble Inn is a classic early 1940s Worcester dining car.

behind the griddle and other work areas. There's even a hand-carved, 3-foot-long scale wooden model of the diner with a roof that flips up so you can peer inside to see likenesses of the counter, stools, booths, and other details. It was built and given to the diner by a regular customer who says it took him three years to complete.

The menu at Daddypop's Tumble Inn is straightforward diner food—bacon, sausage, eggs, pancakes, French toast, burgers, and a variety of sandwiches. The Meat Loaf is outstanding (see page 84), as is the Rueben Omelet, one of Daddypop's more distinctive dishes. If you're there on the right day at the right time, you may be treated to a seranade by the diner's "Singing Chef," James Muskelly Brown,

The official Worcester Dining Car registration plate.

who bursts into song from behind the counter at the least provocation.

The diner is only open for breakfast and lunch, so be sure you arrive by 1 pm so you can enjoy a home-cooked meal and bask in the atmosphere of an old-time diner thriving in the heart of a classic fading yet graceful New England factory town.

MEAT LOAF

DADDYPOP'S TUMBLE INN DINER, CLAREMONT, NH

A classic 1941 Worcester car, Daddypop's Tumble Inn Diner features diner food at its most basic. Try their meat loaf, which is about as basic as it gets. They do it "old school" at Daddypop's—no bread or loaf pan to contain the loaf, just a lump of flavorful meat cooking atop some aluminum foil and set on a cookie sheet. It doesn't get any more basic than that!

2½	pounds ground beef
2	cups bread crumbs
3	eggs, whisked in a small bowl
4	cloves fresh garlic, minced
1	tablespoon white pepper
½	large onion, chopped
½	green bell pepper, chopped

Preheat the oven to 350°F. Thoroughly mix all the ingredients together in a large bowl. Line a cookie sheet with aluminum foil. Form the meat mixture into two loaves. Place each loaf on the foil-lined cookie sheet. Bake for 1 hour and 20 minutes. Remove from oven and let sit before carving slices. Serves 8–10.

NEW ENGLAND BOILED DINNER

There is perhaps no one-pot meal that's as redolent of old-time New England than a New England boiled dinner. Diners throughout the region have been serving this for decades, usually as a special once a week, and it's a favorite of those who know how flavorful and filling it can be. This recipe is adapted from one that appeared in *Yankee Magazine*. It's quick and simple to prepare (not counting the 3-plus hours of cooking time), and it provides great leftovers and an excellent base for Red Flannel Hash (see page 146).

4	pounds ground corned beef	2	turnips, cut into bite-size pieces
15	peppercorns	16	small new potatoes, peeled
8	whole cloves	16	baby carrots, or 4 carrots peeled and cut up
1	bay leaf	8	small white onions
8	small beets	1	head cabbage, cut into 8 wedges

1. In a large pot, cover the corned beef with water and cook, covered, under medium low heat for 10 minutes. Skim off the fat and other residue that forms on top of the water. Add the peppercorns, cloves, and bay leaf. Cover the pot again and simmer for 3 hours or until the meat is tender when prodded with a fork.

2. Place the beets in a separate pan with an inch or so of water. Bring to a boil, then reduce the heat and simmer until tender, about 30 minutes.

3. Add the turnips, potatoes, carrots, and onions to the large pot with the meat. Simmer, covered, for 15 minutes. Add the cabbage wedges and cook, covered, for 15 minutes more. Remove the meat, cut into serving-size pieces, and garnish each plate with vegetables drained from the pot. Serves 12–15.

DOTTIE'S CHICKEN POT PIE

DOTTIE'S DINER, WOODBURY, CT

Housed in a nondescript, upscale strip mall, Dottie's blends into its surroundings visually but not necessarily culinarily. There is some excellent diner food to be had at Dottie's, and one of its most famous and popular dishes is the chicken pot pie. Though you may think, "What's so special about chicken pot pie?" Dottie's rich, warm, filling version will change your mind, with a gravy that goes great on top. This is an excellent winter warmer-upper, but it's good any time of year when you have a hankering for some genuine comfort food.

PIE

1   4-pound chicken

2   sticks celery, chopped

1   medium onion, chopped

1   bay leaf

½   teaspoon salt

¼   teaspoon white pepper

4   carrots, diced into ¼-inch cubes

4   potatoes, diced into ¼-inch cubes

½   cup (1 stick, 4 ounces) butter

½   cup all-purpose flour

½   cup green peas

2   9-inch refrigerated piecrusts

     Salt and pepper to taste

GRAVY

¼   cup onion, chopped

2   tablespoons red peppers, chopped

2   tablespoons green peppers, chopped

4   tablespoons (½ stick, 2 ounces) butter

1   teaspoon jalapeño pepper, chopped

¼   cup all-purpose flour

3   cups water (add chicken base or bullion to taste)

1. Preheat the oven to 375°F. Place the chicken in a large pot and cover with water. Add the chopped celery and onion, bay leaf, salt, and white pepper. Bring to a boil and simmer for 1 hour until done. Strain and save the chicken stock to cook the carrots and potatoes. Set the cooked chicken aside to cool, then pick the meat off the bones and chop into small pieces.

2. Add the carrots and potatoes to the stock and cook until almost tender. Strain the vegetables.

3. In a large pot, melt the butter. Add the flour and salt and pepper to taste. Slowly blend in the stock to the pot to make a cream sauce. Add the chopped chicken, vegetables, and green peas.

4. Before assembling the pie, lightly moisten the rim of one pie shell. Pour the filling into the shell and drape the other pastry over the filling, pressing the top and bottom pastries together along the edge. Trim the pastry flush with the edge of the pan. Using the back of a fork, press the tines along the edge to seal the pastry. Bake for 50 minutes until golden brown and bubbling.

5. To make the gravy, sauté the onions and peppers in the butter. Slowly add the flour and water and cook over low heat, stirring constantly, until brown and thickened to desired consistency. Pour over slices of pie. Serves 4–6.

A Modern Classic

✕ 364 East Avenue
   Pawtucket, RI 02860

☎ 401-726-8390

The Modern Diner's Linguica and Eggs.

The Modern's owner, Nick Demou.

Modern Diner

Few diners in New England draw more high praise from diner aficionados for its architecture and its food than the Modern Diner in the town of Pawtucket, Rhode Island, just north of Providence and south of the border with Massachusetts. After all, back in the late 1970s, the Modern was the first diner to be named to the National Register of Historic Places. It's also now home to one of the best weekend brunches in all of Rhode Island.

The vintage 1941 Sterling Streamliner–style diner was in danger of being demolished in the late 1970s, so in 1978 preservationists lobbied to save it in part by having it placed on the register. The exterior design is striking. With its maroon- and cream-colored façade, the diner is shaped like a classic 1930s *Burlington Zephyr* locomotive streaming down the tracks. And it sports a large neon MODERN DINER sign on the roof.

The Modern was moved from an obscure spot in downtown Pawtucket to a busy street only a few blocks from I-95, which is where it currently resides. The diner was placed on a new foundation, and a new kitchen and second dining room were built on the backside of the diner car. The Demou family purchased the diner in 1986, and Nick Demou, an energetic chef/owner currently in his fifties, has presided over the Modern since his father retired a number of years ago.

A graduate of the culinary school at Johnson & Wales University in Providence, Nick has created a fairly amazing menu over the past couple of decades. It's an interesting mix of traditional diner food and an amazing array of brunch-type omelets, hashes, frittatas, jazzed-up grits, and numerous eggs Benedict dishes. All these intriguing specials are posted daily on laminated signs in the small waiting area between the two dining rooms. On Saturday and Sunday mornings, you'll almost always find a line of customers winding out the door. (Hint: If you're eager to get

The Modern was the first diner in America to be put on the National Register of Historic Places.

seated more quickly, then forego waiting for an open spot in the dining car portion and opt for a table in the rear dining room. The menu is the same, and the food is, of course, every bit as good.)

In terms of diner food, you'll find all the usual suspects: eggs, bacon, sausage, ham, pancakes, and French toast for breakfast; plus meat loaf, beef stew, liver and onions, dogs and beans, burgers, and assorted sandwiches for lunch. A couple of interesting twists are the pancakes covered in the fruit of the day and topped with whipped cream, and the Jimmie Gimmie, a breakfast dish consisting of two poached eggs on an open-faced English muffin with sliced tomatoes, and topped with melted cheese and bacon. If you happen to brave the crowds on the weekends, be sure to get a side order of Linguica Hash, made with spicy Portuguese sausage, which is available on Saturdays and Sundays only.

Here are some of the unique and unusual items you're likely to find on the specials board on any given day and especially on weekends:

☞ Smoked Canadian Bacon, Apple, and Brie Omelet

☞ Lobster Cheese Grits

☞ Sun-Dried Tomato, Caramelized Onion, and Feta Cheese Omelet (see page 23)

☞ Linguica Hash Benedict (don't forget, weekends only)

☞ Spinach, Provolone, and Roasted Red Pepper Omelet

☞ Pesto Cheese Grits and Eggs

☞ Lemon Ricotta Pancakes

And that's just a sampling. There's so much to choose from that you may wish to make some committee decisions with those in your dining party and select items you can all share and sample from each other's plates.

Nick is a tireless innovator in the kitchen, and he loves to see the weekend crowd dig into his specials. If you get the chance, be sure to visit some time on a quiet weekday later in the morning or in the early afternoon, and spend some time soaking in the diner car's old-time atmosphere, with its original tile work, stainless steel backsplash, wooden booths, and wood trim around the curved ceiling. You'll be transported to a different time in this comfortable and warmly lit atmosphere, and you're guaranteed a meal from Nick's kitchen that will not disappoint.

VEGETABLE BEEF STEW

MOODY'S DINER, WALDOBORO, ME

How much more diner can you get than vegetable beef stew? Resist the temptation to do this in the slow cooker. It's much more flavorful when done on the stovetop.

1	pound stew beef, cubed
2	tablespoons Worcestershire sauce
2–3	cups water (approximate)
3	beef bullion cubes
6	medium potatoes, ½-inch dice
½	cup celery, diced
6	medium carrots, sliced
1	14-ounce can stewed tomatoes
1	bay leaf
½	cup frozen peas
	Parsley flakes

1. Braise the beef cubes in a large pot in the Worcestershire sauce. Add water to cover the cubes and cook until tender. Remove the beef from the pot and set aside. Add the bouillon cubes to the pot and dissolve under medium heat. Add the potatoes, celery, carrots, stewed tomatoes, and bay leaf. Then add enough water to cover the vegetables.

2. Bring the stew to a boil, then simmer for 30 minutes. Add the frozen peas in the last 10 minutes. Fold the meat back into the pot along with the parsley flakes and warm over medium-low heat to serving temperature. Serves 6.

Diner Slang

Over the years, an entire vernacular has evolved in American diners that describes diner food, condiments, and activities. These terms were mostly made up by cooks and waitstaff and used as humorous forms of shorthand in the meal-ordering process. This "diner talk" often added verbal color to the experience of eating at a diner, especially for bemused customers sitting at the counter or in nearby booths listening to the exchanges.

The Shawmut Diner in New Bedford, Massachusetts, has kept a running list of these expressions over the years. They hand out the list to customers for their entertainment and edification while waiting for a table or a meal. Here's a sampling:

- **Angels on horseback** Oysters wrapped in bacon and served on toast
- **Atlanta special** Coca-Cola
- **Baled hay** Shredded wheat
- **Belly furniture** Food
- **Blowout patches** Pancakes
- **Canned cow** Evaporated milk
- **C. J. White** Cream cheese and jelly sandwich on white bread
- **Cow paste** Butter
- **Flop two** Two fried eggs, over easy
- **Fry two, let the sun shine** Two fried eggs, sunny-side up
- **Hen Fruit** Egg
- **Hot one** Bowl of chili
- **Hounds on an island** Frankfurters and beans
- **Houseboat** Banana split

- **Life preservers** Doughnuts
- **Mama on a raft** Marmalade on toast
- **Mats** Pancakes
- **Popeye** Spinach
- **Put a hat on it** Add ice cream
- **Rabbit food** Lettuce
- **Raft** Slice of toast
- **Shivering Eve** Apple jelly
- **Sneeze** Pepper
- **Sweep the kitchen** Plate of hash
- **Throw it in the mud** Add chocolate syrup
- **Vermont** Maple syrup
- **Wax** American cheese
- **Wimpy** Hamburger
- **Wrecked hen fruit** Scrambled eggs
- **Yellow paint** Mustard
- **Yum-yum** Sugar

AGAWAM CHICKEN PIES

These hearty chicken pies, best when cooked two at a time, are served at the Agawam with the pies flipped over and served bottom side up with extra gravy on the top. This wonderful recipe appeared in *Saveur* magazine, and it has been adapted here.

PIE

2   Agawam pie doughs (see Piecrust, page 208)

3   large, skin-on chicken breast halves (approximately 2⅔ pounds)

2   carrots, peeled, diced, and boiled until tender

1   cup frozen peas, thawed

GRAVY

4   tablespoons (½ stick, 2 ounces) butter

½   cup all-purpose flour

4   cups reserved chicken broth

1½ tablespoons chicken base (preferably Better Than Bouillon)

Freshly ground black pepper

1. To finish the piecrust, roll each dough disk into a 12-inch circle on a floured countertop or other flat surface. Using a 4 x 6-inch oval casserole dish as a stencil, cut out four ovals of dough and transfer to a floured tray and cover. Set aside.

2. To make the pie filling, put the chicken breast halves into a large pot, cover them with water, adding an extra 2 inches of depth on top, and bring the pot to a boil. Reduce the heat to low and simmer the chicken until almost cooked through, about 15 minutes.

3. Strain the chicken and the broth through a sieve, reserving 4 cups of the broth. Allow the chicken meat to cool to the touch. Remove and discard the chicken skin and bones, and tear the meat into 1- to 2-inch chunks. Set aside.

4. To make the gravy, heat the butter in a saucepan over medium heat. Whisk in the flour and cook, stirring until golden brown, about 2 minutes. Whisk in the reserved 4 cups of broth and bring to a boil. Whisk in the chicken base, allowing the liquid to come to a boil again as you whisk. Reduce the heat to medium low and simmer, stirring occasionally until thickened to a gravy-like consistency, about 40 minutes. Remove the gravy from the heat and season with black pepper to taste.

5. Preheat the oven to 500°F. To assemble the pies, divide the chicken, carrots, and peas evenly into the four casserole dishes. Pour approximately ½ cup of the gravy into each casserole dish, on top of the chicken and vegetables. Top each dish with a dough oval, and tuck in the edges with your fingers or a spoon. Bake until the top is golden brown, about 20 minutes. Remove the pies from the oven, turn them upside down onto plates, and serve with the remaining gravy. Serves 4.

HOMEMADE MEAT LOAF

SONNY'S BLUE BENN DINER, BENNINGTON, VT

The meat loaf at the Blue Benn Diner is a real treat because they dress it up with some nice spices, and they throw in some ground pork with the beef to further broaden the flavor. The use of oatmeal instead of the traditional bread crumbs or crumbled crackers still binds up the loaf very nicely and adds a hint of healthiness.

4	slices bread
1	cup milk
1½	pounds ground beef
½	pound ground pork
1	medium onion, chopped
4	eggs, beaten
¼	cup fresh parsley, chopped
1	tablespoon dried sage
2	teaspoons thyme
1	cup ketchup
¼	cup oatmeal
	Salt to taste

Preheat the oven to 350°F. Mix all the ingredients in a large bowl. Mold the meat into a self-standing loaf shape or pour it into a large bread pan. Bake for about 1 hour or until the inside of the loaf is thoroughly cooked. Drain off the grease, and cut into slices. Serve with mashed potatoes and fresh steamed vegetables. Serves 6.

MOODY'S MEAT LOAF

MOODY'S DINER, WALDOBORO, ME

Though they've fancied up their recipe for meat loaf in recent years at Moody's, old-timers still occasionally ask for the original recipe, as developed by Moody's matriarch, Bertha Moody. This no-nonsense recipe, as presented here, is as simple as it is tasty, and it will transport you to a time when simple and tasty were all that were needed at the family dinner table. (The canned tomato soup over the top is an interesting touch.)

1	pound ground beef
¼	cup onion, finely chopped
6–8	saltine crackers, finely crushed
1	egg
½	cup milk
1	11-ounce can tomato soup
	Salt and pepper to taste

Preheat the oven to 350°F. Combine the ground beef, onions, and saltines. Stir in the egg and milk, adding salt and pepper to taste, until thoroughly mixed. Place the meat mixture in a small, ungreased 5 x 9-inch loaf pan. Bake for 45 minutes. Remove loaf from oven and pour just enough tomato soup over the top to thoroughly cover the loaf. Return to oven and bake for another 45 minutes. Serves 4.

Seafood

New England is blessed with some of the best seafood anywhere—lobsters, clams, haddock, cod, scallops, even the diminutive Maine shrimp. This cornucopia has been on diner menus for decades in straightforward ways (fried clams, lobster rolls, baked haddock) as well as unusual ways (lobster chow mein, finnan haddie, beer-steamed littleneck clams, scallop chowder).

Traditionally the diners closest to the ocean have served up most of the seafood dishes to be found on diner menus in New England. However, with modern transportation, a seafood platter ordered in western New Hampshire can be every bit as good as one consumed on Cape Cod.

The recipes in this chapter celebrate the bounty of the sea and how diners in New England have been serving it up to appreciative customers. Virtually all of these recipes are simple and straightforward, though a few call for unusual ingredients that you may have to procure from a specialty shop or by shopping on the Internet. The most important thing to do is get the freshest seafood you can. This typically costs more, but it makes a huge difference in the outcome of any of these dishes. It may be a hassle to steam or boil and pick your own lobster meat, but the dividends it pays in terms of flavor are enormous. The same goes for fish filets—always go for fresh over previously frozen.

Some of these dishes, like fried clams and lobster chow mein, may turn out better at the diners that serve them regularly, but don't shy away from giving them a try at home. It's only through tinkering in the kitchen that a true appreciation of some of these dishes becomes apparent.

GRANDMOTHER'S LOBSTER PIE

MAINE DINER, WELLS, ME

When brothers Myles and Dick Henry opened the Maine Diner in 1983, they brought along a bunch of their grandmother's recipes. The one that has garnered perhaps the most attention from customers over the years is Grandmother's Lobster Pie. This simple, scrumptious dish is served year-round at the diner and is a favorite of both lunch and dinner patrons. It's easy to make (once you've picked your lobster meat), and the simple list of ingredients belies the dish's fantastic flavor.

4	1-pound lobsters
1	cup (2 sticks, 8 ounces) butter
2	tablespoons lemon juice
1	tube (3 cups) Ritz crackers, crushed
	Parsley
	Lemon wedges

1. Preheat the oven to 425°F. Steam the lobsters 12–15 minutes in salted water, or until done. Cool. Over a bowl, to retain the juices, pick out the meat from the tails, knuckles, and claws. Reserve the tomalley (the lobster's liver, a greenish substance). Melt the butter in a frying pan. Stir in the tomalley and lemon juice. Remove from heat. Stir the crushed Ritz crackers into the tomalley mixture. Add enough reserved lobster juice until the mixture is moist and thick, like turkey stuffing.

2. Divide the lobster meat among four individual casserole dishes. Cover the meat with the cracker mixture, patting it on evenly. Bake until the tops begin to brown—about 10 minutes. Garnish with parsley and lemon wedges. Serves 4.

COD CAKES

MAINE DINER, WELLS, ME

These pan-fried fish-and-potato patties make for a wonderful wintertime seafood entrée. Remember, the fresher the cod, the better the cakes.

Butter

1 small onion, finely chopped

2 tablespoons (¼ stick, 1 ounce) butter

1 pound salt cod, diced

3 pounds mashed potatoes

1 teaspoon pepper

2 eggs, beaten

Vegetable or other cooking oil (enough to thoroughly coat a frying pan to a depth of ¼ inch)

1. Sauté the onion in butter in a pan. Place the remaining ingredients in a bowl, adding the eggs last, and mix thoroughly. Let the mixture set in the refrigerator overnight.

2. Heat the cooking oil in a pan. Form the cod cakes into small, 3-ounce patties, and place them carefully in the hot cooking oil. Cook on one side for 3 minutes, then turn over and cook until golden brown. Makes 24 cakes.

GRILLED SEA SCALLOPS WITH HORSERADISH SAUCE

Not all kitchens are equipped with a grill, but this flavorful seafood dish may be done in a cast-iron skillet or on a stovetop griddle or outdoor grill, as long as you keep a watchful eye on the scallops while they're cooking. The simple horseradish sauce is the perfect complement to the mild-flavored scallops, and it's super easy to make.

HORSERADISH SAUCE

- 2 tablespoons freshly ground horseradish
- 4 tablespoons mayonnaise
- Dash of hot sauce to taste

SCALLOPS

- 2 teaspoons vegetable oil
- ½ teaspoon salt
- ½ teaspoon basil
- ½ teaspoon thyme
- ¼ teaspoon garlic powder
- ¼ teaspoon onion powder
- 1 pound medium sea scallops
- Lemon wedges

1. To make the horseradish sauce, mix all the ingredients together in a small bowl and set aside so the flavors can bond.

2. To prepare the scallops, preheat the grill or pan and coat lightly with the vegetable oil. In a small bowl, combine the salt, basil, thyme, garlic powder, and onion powder. Pat the sea scallops dry, then sprinkle the spice mixture on both sides of the scallops.

3. Place the scallops on the preheated grill or skillet, and sear for 3–4 minutes on one side until they're golden brown. Carefully turn the scallops over with tongs and cook on the other side for 2–3 minutes, again until golden brown. Be careful not to overcook. Serve with dollops of the horseradish sauce and garnish with lemon wedges. Serves 4–5.

It's a Wonderful Life at the Maine Diner

✕ 2265 Post Road
Wells, ME 04090

☎ 207-646-4441

① www.mainediner.com

The Main Diner's bright roadside sign pulls 'em in.

Maine Diner

It all began on a cold and snowy morning in February 1983. Brothers Dick and Myles Henry had just opened their newly christened Maine Diner on US 9 in the town of Wells. Their first customer arrived with a bang, drunkenly driving into a pole by the restaurant, which the driver may have mistaken for a local bar. The inebriated customer stopped in, sobered up with a couple cups of coffee, and had the first meal served by the Myleses in their new establishment.

Thirty years and 6 million customers later, the Maine Diner is still at it—and it's bigger and better than ever. Known for locally, even nationally famous dishes such as Lobster Pie (see page 98), Cod Cakes (see page 99), and Myles Henry's classic Seafood Chowder (see page 50), this southern Maine institution almost always has a line out the door.

The Maine Diner doesn't necessarily sport the classic diner look. It's housed in a spacious, flat-roofed, one-story, white frame building with blue-and-white awnings around the front and sides, and it has a colorful sign on a big pole right out front (not the pole struck by the first customer). There's a gift shop in a house-like building next door. In back of the restaurant are approximately 2 acres of vegetable gardens where much of the diner's produce comes from when in season.

The gardens are a legacy of the diner's original owner, Socrates "Louie" Toton, who had a diner in Boston and purchased the then-named Maine Restaurant in the 1950s as a sort of plaything to run in his retirement years. In almost counterintuitive fashion, Toton kept his diner open September through May and closed down for the summer months, presumably so that he could focus his attention on the gardens out back. Anyone who owns a business in Maine knows that the three best reasons to do so are June, July, and August. So, although Socrates's restaurant wasn't a moneymaker, it seemed to keep the retiree content in its own idiosyncratic way.

Enter the Brothers Henry in 1983. After their first customer ate his oatmeal, paid his bill, and went on his way, the Maine Diner served some 40 more customers that day. The next day they served 100 customers, and they haven't looked back since.

Breakfast is served at any time and features the usual eggs, omelets, bacon, eggs, homefries, and toast. In addition, there's a whole rainbow of specialty dishes, such as Maine Crab Benedict, Eggs Florentine, Lobster Quiche, and a breakfast burrito that's more than enough for two hungry people.

They started with a simple menu that they inherited from Socrates, supplementing it with some dishes from their parents' and grandmother's kitchens. Then they slowly, steadily expanded the menu until they had the full array of dishes that currently appear either regularly or cyclically as specials.

Where to begin? Seafood is probably the best place. The Maine Diner's Lobster Pie and Seafood Chowder are nationally renowned. Their deep-fried clams and cod cakes are light, crispy, and perfectly cooked in clean, high-grade vegetable oil. Actually, you can't go wrong with any platter of seafood that you might order here. Haddock comes baked or fried or baked and stuffed, and it's as fresh as can be—light and flaky with a mild white fish flavor (see Baked Haddock, page 106).

On the diner side of things, there's homemade mac and cheese; open-faced turkey and roast beef sandwiches served with mashed potatoes and a signature Maine Diner corn muffin; chili; chicken pot pie; and the Thursday special New England boiled dinner.

Perhaps the best and most distinguishing thing about the Maine Diner is the friendly, unflappable service delivered by the experienced waitstaff, some of whom have been working at the Maine for decades. The busy, crowded dining room is always infused with warmth, smiles, and helpful hands eager to make your meal at the Maine Diner as satisfying and memorable as it can be. Six million customers (and counting) can't be wrong.

The expansive garden in back provides much of the diner's fresh produce.

SHRIMP, SCALLOPS, PEAS, PROSCIUTTO, AND SUN-DRIED TOMATOES OVER PENNE

SEAPLANE DINER, PROVIDENCE, RI

This cornucopia of seafood, vegetables, prosciutto, and pasta is a very popular weekend special at the Seaplane. The recipe was invented by one of the diner's chefs, Mynor Recinos, and it combines a whole lot of healthy and flavorful ingredients into a hearty and satisfying one-dish seafood dinner.

1 pound dry penne pasta	¼ pound prosciutto, finely chopped
2 cloves fresh garlic, chopped	¼ cup sun-dried tomatoes, chopped
4 tablespoons olive oil	2 cups marinara sauce (homemade, if you can; otherwise, prepared marinara will do)
4 tablespoons (½ stick, 2 ounces) butter	
½ teaspoon granulated garlic	¼ cup heavy cream
½ teaspoon onion powder	½ cup fresh parsley, finely chopped
2 pounds (16–24 count) raw shrimp, shelled	Fresh grated Parmesan cheese
1 pound fresh sea scallops	Black pepper to taste
½ cup frozen green peas, thawed	

1. Bring a pot of salted water to boil, and cook the penne until it's al dente. Drain the penne and set it aside in a large serving bowl.

2. In a large saucepan or pot, sauté the garlic, olive oil, butter, granulated garlic, and onion powder over low heat to make a garlic butter mixture. Add the shrimp, scallops, peas, prosciutto, and sun-dried tomatoes. Continue to cook over low heat, stirring gently for several minutes to let the seafood cook most of the way through.

3. Stir in the marinara sauce and the heavy cream. Bring to a low boil and let it bubble for 4 minutes to reduce the sauce and combine the flavors. Add black pepper to taste, and stir in the chopped parsley just before removing from heat.

4. Pour the sauce over the cooked penne in the serving bowl, gently stirring to combine the ingredients, and serve with fresh grated Parmesan or other hard Italian cheese. Serves 6.

BAKED HADDOCK

MAINE DINER, WELLS, ME

Nothing says Friday dinner in New England like baked haddock. This tasty, easy-to-prepare dish utilizes one of the region's most underrated fish—and one that's increasing in importance as the stocks of cod off New England's coastline continue to dwindle. Feel free to dress up this dish with any herbs or seasonings that strike your fancy.

2   pounds fresh haddock fillets

3   tablespoons (⅜ stick, 1½ ounces) butter, melted

1   tablespoon lemon juice

1   tube (3 cups) Ritz crackers, ground into crumbs

2   tablespoons fresh parsley, finely chopped

1   tablespoon paprika

Preheat the oven to 400°F. Place the haddock fillets in a casserole dish and top with butter and lemon juice. Sprinkle the cracker crumbs over the top, then sprinkle the chopped parsley and paprika on top of the cracker crumbs. Bake uncovered for 12–14 minutes until fillets flake at the touch of a fork. Serves 4.

LOBSTER CHOW MEIN

EVELYN'S DRIVE IN, TIVERTON, RI

This unusual dish has been featured on Guy Fieri's *Diners, Drive-Ins and Dives*, and with good reason. It's one of the most unusual and alluring dishes you'll find at any New England roadside diner. It dates back to the beginning of Evelyn's Drive-In in eastern Rhode Island, and it makes use of some interesting local ingredients, most notably the crispy chow mein noodles and the mysterious, exotic Hoo-Me Gravy Mix, both of which come from the Oriental Chow Mein Company, a small manufacturer in nearby Fall River, Massachusetts (both are available online). The dish can be a bit of an acquired taste, but the locals love it, and chances are you will, too.

2 1-pound lobsters *or*	1 Spanish onion, wedged
½ pound lobster meat	2–3 stalks celery, cut into 1-inch-long strips
½ gallon water	4–5 fresh mushrooms, sliced
1 16-ounce can chicken broth	1 cup fresh bean sprouts
1 tablespoon chicken base	2 tablespoons Hoo-Mee Gravy Mix
1 tablespoon salt	Crispy chow mein noodles (*not* the soft, lo mein–style noodles)
1 teaspoon black pepper	

1. Boil or steam lobsters until cooked. Set aside to cool, then pick the meat out of the shells. Bring the water and chicken broth to a boil, then add the chicken base, salt, and pepper. Add the vegetables and cook until the celery is tender. Add the gravy mix to the pot and stir to thicken.

2. Place a handful of the chow mein noodles in a serving bowl, and ladle the vegetable-and-gravy mix over the noodles. Top with chunks of fresh lobster meat and bean sprouts. Serves 3–4.

A Little Slice of Heaven on Nanaquaket Pond

2335 Main Road
Tiverton, RI 02878

☎ 401-624-3100

ⓘ www.evelynsdrivein.com

Evelyn's co-owners, Jane and Domenic Bitto.

Evelyn's Drive-In

Evelyn's has been around in one form or another since 1969, when Evelyn Dupont opened her unusual hybrid eatery in eastern Rhode Island on US 77, tucked along the shore of Nanaquaket Pond in the town of Tiverton. Equal parts diner and clam shack, this little gem remained a secret to most of the world until it was featured on *Diners, Drive-Ins and Dives* several years ago. By that time Evelyn had retired and sold the restaurant to Domenic and Jane Bitto, a wide-eyed couple with little experience in the restaurant business who bought the place in the early 1990s.

The Bittos initially stuck close to Evelyn's original menu, and they have steadily added their own creations over the years. On the diner side of the menu, there's Evelyn's famous meat loaf and chicken pie, both done in classic diner style and each coming with generous helpings of homemade mashed potatoes and steamed fresh, locally grown vegetables.

Seafood is what this place is really known for, and the most unusual dish (and one of the most popular) is the Lobster Chow Mein (see page 107). An Evelyn Dupont original, this item has been on the menu for decades and features generous chunks of fresh-picked lobster meat on a pile of crispy, crunchy chow mein noodles with a ladle of glutinous chow mein gravy covering the entire dish. Lobster Chow Mein is a curious combination of flavors and textures, and if you're feeling adventurous, give it a try. Lots of people love it and come back for it repeatedly.

Also high on the seafood list here are the fried whole-belly clams. They're sweet and crunchy and full of briny, whole-clam flavor. The other deep-fried local seafood treats, such as scallops, clam strips, and fish and chips, are also outstanding.

There are three different ways to dine at Evelyn's, each with its own special appeal. First, there's the order window on the front of the little

Evelyn's on a sunny summer day.

red building, where you may place your order and pick up your food if you wish to dine in the rough. You may then grab one of the covered picnic tables along the edge of the pond and dig in.

For the diner experience, step inside the red shack, where you'll find a small counter and several tables, an intimate setting similar to what you'll find in any cozy diner anywhere. There's a sign next to the order window between kitchen and counter that reads IF YOU'RE IN A HURRY, YOU'RE IN THE WRONG PLACE. This is a testament to the restaurant's relaxed, serene atmosphere. Once you settle in at Evelyn's, you're going to want to linger.

If you walk through the indoor dining area and out the back door, you'll find yourself on a crushed-shell patio area with a dozen or so tables overlooking the pond. Table service is the method of ordering out here, with several servers watching over diners'

needs, taking food orders, delivering a wide variety of libations (Evelyn's has a full liquor license), and chatting with customers as they come and go. This is the preferred place to be when the sun is setting over the pond. It's a peaceful, Zen-like experience to watch birds skim over the water and small watercraft glide by while the sun slowly disappears behind the opposite shore.

Dessert is celebrated at Evelyn's with their famous Grape-Nut Pudding (see page 168), home-baked apple and blueberry pies, Buddha's Chocolate (a Jane Bitto creation; see page 185), and Evelyn's rich, caloric Brownie Sundae.

So, if you can't decide whether you want a dine-in-the-rough seafood experience or the comfort of a diner, head over to Evelyn's where you may experience both under one roof *and* under the stars.

FRIED CLAMS

MAINE DINER, WELLS, ME

Normally it makes more sense to go out for fried whole-belly clams and let the experts with the deep fryers and other specialized equipment do the work while you enjoy the fruits of their labors and come home to a clean kitchen. However, you can fry up clams at home if you want, and the Maine Diner has an excellent recipe that mirrors how they do it (and they do it very well) at their fine establishment.

4	eggs
1	cup milk
2	cups all-purpose flour
2	cups cornmeal
6	cups canola oil
2	pounds fresh-shucked frying clams

1. In a bowl, beat the 4 eggs. Add the milk and beat some more. In a shallow dish, mix the flour and cornmeal until well blended.

2. In a large pot, heat the canola oil under medium-high heat until it reaches 365°F. Take a quarter (½ pound) of the clams and dip in the egg wash. Then place them in the flour mixture and thoroughly coat each clam. Put the clams in a strainer and thoroughly shake off the excess flour.

3. Carefully place the clams in the hot oil and cook until golden brown. They don't take long to brown up, so watch them carefully. Remove them from the oil and place them on a paper bag or paper towels for a couple of minutes to cool a bit and let the oil drain off.

4. Repeat the process for the remaining three batches of clams. Serves 4–6.

BEER-STEAMED LITTLENECK CLAMS

EVELYN'S DRIVE-IN, TIVERTON, RI

A bunch of steamed clams served with drawn butter or clam broth can be a heavenly appetizer. And they're even better when steamed in a broth of salsa, olive oil, garlic—and beer! Try this simple, tasty method of steaming clams for a little extra flavor and zing.

2	dozen littleneck clams
1	16-ounce jar salsa (any commercial brand is fine)
¼	cup olive oil
3	cloves fresh garlic, chopped
1	12-ounce bottled beer (any brand or type is fine)

Mix all the ingredients together with the littlenecks in a large pot. Cover and cook gently over medium heat until the clamshells open. Be careful not to overcook. Serves 3–4.

FINNAN HADDIE

BECKY'S DINER, PORTLAND, ME

This traditional Scottish dish of smoked haddock is popular in certain pockets of Maine, most notably Stonington up near Mount Desert Island. Becky's Diner also does a nice Finnan Haddie as an occasional special.

3	pounds smoked Atlantic haddock fillets
4–6	potatoes, mashed
2	hard-boiled eggs, sliced

WHITE SAUCE

1	white onion, diced
½	stick butter
¼	cup all-purpose flour
1	cup fish stock
	Salt and pepper to taste

1. To prepare the smoked haddock, in a large pot, cover with water and boil for 1 hour. Drain the fish (saving 1 cup of the water to use as fish stock), then boil for another 10 minutes in clean water. Drain the fillets again, then remove the bones.

2. To make the white sauce, sauté the white onion in the butter. When the onion is translucent, add the flour, stir, and cook for another 3 minutes. Add the fish stock, then salt and pepper to taste.

3. Combine the smoked haddock with the white sauce and serve over individually plated spoonfuls of mashed potatoes. Top with sliced hard-boiled eggs. Serves 6. (Peas make a nice side dish.)

LOBSTER AND JUMBO SHRIMP LINGUINE

RUTH AND WIMPY'S, HANCOCK, ME

Ruth and Wimpy Wilbur, owners of Ruth and Wimpy's Kitchen in Hancock, Maine, have over 150 items on their menu, including 30 different lobster dishes. Ruth claims that one of their most popular items is the Lobster and Jumbo Shrimp Linguine, a belly-busting plate of seafood and pasta soaked in garlic, butter, white sauce, and wine. The Wilburs are big on lobster claw meat; but if you find it difficult to procure enough claw meat affordably, feel free to supplement or substitute with chopped tail or knuckle meat. This is a great year-round dish, and the fresher the lobster, the better the results!

1 pound linguine or fettuccine

4 tablespoons (½ stick, 2 ounces) butter

4 teaspoons fresh garlic, chopped

12 fresh-picked lobster claws (or equivalent in tail and knuckle meat)

12 cooked jumbo shrimp, deveined and butterflied

4 cups white sauce (see below)

¼ cup white wine

4 teaspoons shaved cheddar cheese

Salt and pepper to taste

WHITE SAUCE

6 tablespoons (¾ stick, 3 ounces) butter

⅜ cup all-purpose flour

3 cups milk

1. To prepare the pasta, cook the linguine or fettuccine in a pot of boiling salted water. At the same time, melt the butter in a large skillet. Briefly sauté the garlic in the butter, then add and gently sauté the lobster meat and jumbo shrimp.

2. To make the white sauce, melt the butter in a saucepan over medium heat. Blend in the flour and whisk or stir until well combined. Slowly pour in the milk, whisking or stirring constantly as the sauce thickens. Add more milk if the sauce is too thick.

3. Blend the white sauce and white wine into the lobster and shrimp skillet mixture and simmer until bubbling. Season with salt and pepper to taste. Add the shaved cheddar cheese, then pour the sauce over the cooked linguine or fettuccine. Serves 4–5.

A Providence Classic

✕ 307 Allens Avenue
Providence, RI 02905

☎ 401-941-9547

Seaplane Diner

Providence, Rhode Island, is the birthplace of the American diner, and though the Seaplane Diner can't claim to be the first, it can certainly claim to be one of the best of the numerous diners currently in the city.

The Seaplane debuted as Girard's Diner in the northern Rhode Island town of Woonsocket in 1949. Designed and built by the Jerry O'Mahony Company of New Jersey, the diner stayed in Woonsocket for 25 years or so before being moved by Bob and Mike Arena to its current location in 1973. At various times, its original exterior was covered over with different materials and designs, but when current owner Dave Penta took over in the late 1990s, he restored the original stainless steel exterior, which is kept nice and shiny to this day.

Dining at the Seaplane is as authentic a diner experience as you'll get anywhere. When you climb up the several stairs and enter through the glassed-in foyer, you're greeted by a long counter and about a dozen booths done up in bright blue and yellow Naugahyde and blue Formica-topped tables. The counter and stools sport the same blue-and-yellow motif. Large windows look out on the traffic whizzing by on Allens Avenue and on the aging shipyards across the street. (The diner's name comes from the seaplanes that used to land in the harbor across the street from the diner.) The neighborhood is industrial, but many feel with the recent renaissance in downtown Providence to the north, it's only a matter of time before this old factory and port district becomes gentrified.

The Seaplane's menu is about as diner as it gets. Breakfast is all eggs, bacon, sausage, omelets, pancakes, French toast, and waffles. The spicy Portuguese linguiça (pronounced ling-GWEES) sausage is the preferred side-dish meat for those looking for something a bit more adventurous.

Lunch consists of mostly sandwiches, many with Italian American roots, such as the Italian Sausage and Sweet Peppers, the Meatball

It's easy to spot the Seaplane Diner, with its distinctive roof art.

Parmigiana, and the deep-fried Veal or Chicken Parmigiana, each smothered in a tasty homemade tomato sauce and mozzarella cheese. As if the immense sandwiches aren't enough, each comes with a generous helping of French fries and coleslaw, all at very affordable prices.

The dinner menu is split pretty evenly between meat-and-potato specials and surprisingly fresh seafood. Roast turkey, a diner mainstay, is served daily with mashed potatoes, stuffing, cranberry sauce, and vegetables. The meat loaf dinner comes with a thick slab of very tasty loaf accompanied by mashed potatoes, vegetables, and a generous ladling of beef gravy over the meat and potatoes. The chicken and veal parmigiana reappear on the evening menu, only in full-plate form with penne pasta and vegetables on the side.

Owner Dave Penta is particularly proud of his clam cakes, and he should be. A half dozen make for a great appetizer when shared by two or more diners. (Be careful, they'll fill you up.) There's a wonderful seafood platter filled with fresh delicacies from the sea for a very affordable price. Deep-fried whole-belly clams and fish and chips are other great choices. There's also a fresh-baked scrod with white wine, butter, lemon, and a crushed Ritz cracker–crumb topping for those who wish to stay away from deep-fried fare.

One more thing to mention about the Seaplane—less than a mile down the road to the south is Johnson & Wales University's Culinary Arts Museum (see page 38), which has a wonderful, walk-through exhibit detailing the history of diners in America. If you really want to do it right, check out the diner exhibit, then motor up to the Seaplane to get your diner food fix. What you learn at the museum will make your Seaplane Diner experience that much more enjoyable.

LOBSTER STEW

Lobster stew is a classic Maine dish. It's served up at only a few diners in New England and is perhaps done best by the crew at the Maine Diner. Resembling a thick, rich soup rather than a stew, it tastes best when some of the lobster's green-colored tomalley is added to the cooking pot.

It's simple to make—once you've picked your lobster meat. Boil or steam up a good-size lobster, round up the few other ingredients needed, and get ready for a rich, rewarding bowlful of lobster goodness.

1 whole 1½-pound hardshell lobster	½ teaspoon tomalley (the lobster's liver, a greenish substance in the body cavity)
1 quart half-and-half	
1 cup milk	Pinch of paprika
½ cup (1 stick, 4 ounces) butter	Salt and pepper to taste
	Oyster crackers

1. Bring a large pot with water to boil or steam, and cook the lobster for 15 minutes, until the outer shell is crimson. Remove the cooked lobster from the pot, set aside, and let cool for 15 minutes. Crack open the claws, knuckles, and tail, and pick out the lobster meat. Locate the green-colored tomalley (liver) in the lobster's main cavity, scoop it out, and set aside.

2. In a separate pot over medium heat, combine all the ingredients except the lobster and heat until steaming but not boiling. Turn the heat down to low and simmer for 1–2 minutes. Add the lobster meat, stir until well blended, turn off the heat, add salt and pepper to taste, let stand for several minutes,, and serve with oyster crackers. Serves 3–4.

Interesting Entrées

The majority of diners in New England usually don't stray very far from the standard dishes that have appeared on their menus since the mid-1900s. There's great comfort in the consistency these places provide to their communities and their regular customers. But mixing up the formula in a diner's kitchen can often lead to interesting results.

There are several diners in New England, such as O'Rourke's in Connecticut and A1 in Maine, that routinely step outside the boundaries of traditional diner fare, and this chapter features a handful of recipes from such places that either riff on classic diner dishes or that break new ground completely.

A few of these recipes straddle the border of straight-up diner food, like American Chop Suey, Shepherd's Pie, and variations on the mac and cheese and grilled cheese themes. A few others introduce exotic or unusual ingredients that you wouldn't expect to find in the arsenal of your typical diner. All of this creative cookery is done in the spirit of adventure to satisfy curious customers who love diners and who crave culinary experimentation at the same time.

These recipes offer just a sampling of all the interesting nontraditional entrées out there; in most cases, they're contemporary dishes with strong roots in the diner cuisine tradition. From lamb to Brie to chouriço to chimichurri sauce, there are some fun things to check out here. Have a good time with these recipes and be sure to visit these diners to see what they're up to on any given day. You're almost certainly in for some pleasant surprises.

AMERICAN CHOP SUEY

AGAWAM DINER, ROWLEY, MA

Here's a great recipe from the Agawam Diner that appeared in a slightly different form in *Saveur* magazine several years ago. American Chop Suey, or "American Chop," as it's often referred to in diner-speak, is more Italian and Mexican than it is Chinese. Try this one out on a cold winter's night when you've got a crowd of hungry people gathered around the table. You'll be praised for your culinary prowess, even though this dish is a snap to throw together.

3	tablespoons olive oil		1	teaspoon crushed red pepper flakes
3	tablespoons (⅜ stick, 1½ ounces) butter		1	28-ounce can whole peeled tomatoes
1	medium yellow onion, finely chopped		2	15-ounce cans tomato sauce
1	medium green bell pepper, finely chopped		2	teaspoons sugar
1	pound ground beef		¼	teaspoon ground cinnamon
2	teaspoons garlic powder		1	pound dried elbow macaroni
2	teaspoons onion powder			Salt and pepper to taste
1	teaspoon paprika			

1. Heat the olive oil and the butter in a large pot over medium-high heat. Add the chopped onion and bell pepper and cook until softened, about 8–10 minutes. Add the ground beef, garlic powder, onion powder, paprika, crushed red pepper flakes, and salt and pepper to taste. Cook, stirring occasionally, until the meat is lightly browned.

2. Add the whole peeled tomatoes and crush with a potato masher (or with your hands before adding them to the pot). Add the two cans of tomato sauce, the sugar, and the cinnamon, and stir until thoroughly mixed. Bring the pot to a boil, then reduce the heat and simmer, stirring occasionally, until the sauce thickens, about 45 minutes.

3. In the meantime, bring a large pot of water to boil. Add the elbow macaroni and stir occasionally until cooked al dente. Drain and rinse the macaroni in cold water. Fold the cooked macaroni into the pot of sauce, and mix well. Season with salt and pepper to taste, and simmer for 10 minutes to let the flavors come together. Serves 6.

LOBSTER AND BRIE GRILLED CHEESE

BLUE PLATE DINER, MIDDLETOWN, RI

Only the upscale Blue Plate Diner could come up with such a fancy version of grilled cheese. Fresh-picked lobster meat is the key to this delicacy. You're going to make a lobster salad to pile onto the bread slices, so if you have an alternative lobster salad recipe, feel free to use it. Also, you don't have to use a fancy Brie for this sandwich to work to full effect, but the nicer the Brie, the smoother the overall flavor. This can make a nice dinner entrée with a chowder and perhaps some oven-roasted potatoes on the side.

1   whole 1½-pound lobster, cooked, shelled, and chilled

½   cup mayonnaise

1   teaspoon tarragon

Juice of half a lemon

Salt and pepper to taste

Butter

8   slices brioche bread or Texas toast

1   cup Brie cheese, cut into thin slices (rind is okay)

1. Preheat a griddle or large skillet to 325°F. In a large bowl, combine the lobster meat, mayonnaise, tarragon, and lemon juice. Season with salt and pepper to taste. Spread soft, whole butter on the bread slices, then place 4 pieces of bread onto the griddle or skillet, butter side down. Place two slices of Brie onto the pieces of toasting bread, then top the cheese with the lobster mixture.

2. Cook for 4 minutes before topping each open-faced sandwich with another piece of bread. Flip the sandwiches and cook, covered, for 2 minutes, flipping once more to even out the browning. The lobster mixture should be slightly warmed and the Brie melted. Serves 4.

ASPARAGUS MAC AND CHEESE

A1 DINER, GARDINER, ME

Want to add a bit of extra flavor and nutrition to your mac and cheese? Try slicing up some fresh asparagus and adding it to the mix. Mike Giberson's version of the mac and cheese classic allows you to select whatever cheese you wish, which gives you an amazing number of additional variations on this tried-and-true diner favorite. And the asparagus is the icing on the mac and cheese cake, giving it an earthy flavor and a shot of green veggie goodness at the same time.

1	pound dry macaroni		3	tablespoons all-purpose flour
1	pound fresh asparagus, trimmed and cut into 1½-inch pieces		½	teaspoon white pepper
2½	cups milk		1	cup assorted cheeses, shredded
6	tablespoons (¾ stick, 3 ounces) butter			Salt and pepper to taste

1. In a large pot, heat 6 quarts of salted water to a boil. Drop the macaroni in, stir, and cook to your desired degree of doneness for pasta. Drain and set aside.

2. Blanch the asparagus in boiling water for 5 minutes. Drain and cool it immediately in a bowl of cold water. Drain again and set it aside.

3. Warm the milk, but do not let it boil. Melt the butter in a stainless steel saucepan on medium-low heat. Whisk the flour into the butter and cook, stirring for 2–3 minutes, reducing the heat so the flour/butter roux mixture does not get dark. Add the warm milk in increments and whisk it as you do so.

4. Once the mixture has thickened and is starting to give off wisps of steam, add all the cheese and stir until melted. Add salt and pepper to taste. Add the asparagus pieces, pour over the cooked pasta, mix well, and serve. Or, you can put the asparagus mac and cheese in a casserole dish and brown the top under the broiler for 1–2 minutes. Serves 4–6.

Giberson's Garden of Eden

✕ 3 Bridge Street
  Gardiner, ME 04345

☎ 207-582-4804

① www.a1diner.com

A1 Diner owner and head chef Mike Giberson.

Fish tacos.

A1 Diner

At first glance, the A1 Diner in Gardiner, Maine, looks like a streetcar stopping at curbside to pick up riders. It sits hard by Bridge Street on its steel supports that keep the rail car–style building propped up some 30 feet above a creek-side road and parking lot. This diner's unusual and extraordinary physical characteristics reflect the unusual and extraordinary cuisine that owner Michael Giberson and his staff cook up at the A1 on a daily basis. If originality of cuisine, quality of ingredients, and care in preparation factor highly in your evaluation and appreciation of fine diners and diner food, then the A1 is one of the finest diners you'll find anywhere. It's one of those rare spots that's worth driving dozens, even a hundred miles or more out of your way to experience.

The diner first opened as Heald's in 1946 (the Heald's name still appears on the front of the building). Like most diners of its day, it served large portions of wholesome food at affordable prices to workers who toiled in the local mills and factories. As with so many New England towns, the mills and factories shut down or moved away, but the diner hung in there and kept adapting to local needs and trends. In 1988, current owners Michael Giberson and Neil Andersen purchased the eatery from Michael's father, Al "Gibby" Giberson. (Michael had worked beside his father at the diner in years past.) They renamed it the A1 Diner, and they set off on a path that has made the A1 a regionally and nationally famous restaurant.

The diner itself is a classic 1946 Worcester model (number 790, to be precise), manufactured in Massachusetts, then shipped up to Gardiner for assembly and placement on the iron stilts. Inside the diner, you'll find virtually all the original tile work and many of the original fixtures. Despite the precariousness of the stilts, this is a solid edifice with a marble countertop, booths and woodwork made of heavy oak, chrome-plated counter stools, and many other charming touches. The

The A1 Diner in autumn.

The A1 features a beautifully restored 1940s Worcester dining car interior.

windows that cover the lengths of three sides of the diner make the A1 brighter and cheerier than many diners of similar vintage. Even on a cloudy day, the place is radiant.

There are two types of cuisine on the A1 menu: the basic diner fare, and everything else, much of which tends to be on the exotic side, by diner standards. Diner purists may be put off by the latter fare, which usually appears in the form of daily specials, but it's these specials that really make the A1 stand out as a diner of distinction.

Eggs, omelets, pancakes, waffles, French toast, and sides like homefries and corned beef hash dominate the breakfast offerings. (The corned beef hash, by the way, was recently renamed Bob's Corned Beef Hash after longtime employee Bob Newell, who cooked the hash and many other items at the diner for over 50 years before retiring.)

One of the more popular dishes at lunchtime is the fresh-ground burger, made with locally raised beef, and accompanied with hand-cut French fries. Additionally, there are all the usual sandwich choices, such as Reubens, club sandwiches, and grilled cheese, including a very nice grilled Gruyère cheese sandwich with caramelized onions.

Dinnertime features baked beans with franks, a huge helping of mac and cheese, meat loaf, fried clams, pot roast, and nicely grilled pork chops, served two at a time with applesauce.

It's virtually impossible to characterize the specials at the A1. They are as varied as they are excellent. Giberson and his crew draw on all sorts of culinary influences for their soups, salads, mains, sides, and desserts. The best way to glimpse what's going on in the A1's kitchen is to "like" their Facebook page, where there are daily postings with photographs of what's cooking that day. For example, here's what was featured in a recent week: Syrian cod cakes in a spiced tomato sauce; red, white, and black bean chili; spinach with dates, red onions, and sumac-smoked pita; lemon pudding cake; grilled turkey, Brie, and apple butter; lamb with eggplant curry and jasmine rice; and coffee tapioca pudding. It's certainly not your standard diner fare, but it's oh, so good.

It's been 25 years since Giberson took the reins from his father, and the A1 continues to reinvent itself on an almost daily basis. Lock this place into your GPS and pay a visit as soon as you can. On any given day, there's almost certainly going to be a dish or two served up at the A1 that'll take your breath away.

DINAH'S SHEPHERD'S PIE

RED ARROW DINER, MANCHESTER, NH

It gets cold in New Hampshire in wintertime, and hearty fare is highly sought after to keep the engine running, especially for those who brave the elements and work outdoors during the cold and snowy months. Shepherd's pie, a comfort food dish brought to us by our friends in England, is a popular wintertime item at the Red Arrow Diner, especially with its trademark Flavor-Glow sprinkling over the top.

1	pound ground beef
1	pound mashed potatoes (homemade is best; any recipe is fine)
¼	cup onion, diced
1	teaspoon fresh garlic, chopped
½	teaspoon garlic salt
1	teaspoon black pepper
1	teaspoon granulated onion powder
1	teaspoon Flavor-Glow beef soup base (available online) or other beef soup base
1	8-ounce can creamed corn
1	8-ounce can whole corn kernels

Preheat the oven to 350°F. In a skillet, brown the ground beef, onions, and spices. Drain. Spread evenly in a 9 x 13-inch baking dish. Mix the creamed corn and the corn kernels together and layer on top of the hamburger and onions. Layer the mashed potatoes on top of the corn, smooth them out, then sprinkle the Flavor-Glow on top. Bake, uncovered, for 20 minutes. Refrigerate until cool, then slice into 9–12 pieces. Serves 6–8.

CHOURIÇO AND PEPPERS

This dish is a nod to the Portuguese communities in eastern Rhode Island and southeastern Massachusetts, where the chouriço (pronounced shore-EEEZ) sausage is a staple in the local diet. The simplicity and spiciness of this recipe makes it a favorite main-course dish year-round. The chouriço is ground up prior to cooking, so this doesn't have the look of your typical sausage dish. You may wish to consider serving it on a toasted Portuguese hard roll as a sandwich, like they do at Evelyn's.

2   pounds ground chouriço sausage

1   jar spaghetti sauce (any commercial brand will do)

1   large green bell pepper, chopped (not too small)

2   teaspoons pimenta moída (a Portuguese pepper sauce, available online and in specialty shops)

Combine all the ingredients in a slow cooker and cook on low heat for 6–8 hours. Serves 6.

KICK'D UP MAC 'N CHEESE

BLUE PLATE DINER, MIDDLETOWN, RI

Wintertime in New England calls for comfort food, and baked macaroni and cheese in all its classic and contemporary variations is just the thing to warm you up on a cold winter's day. This version, from Ted Karousos's Blue Plate Diner, just outside Newport, Rhode Island, calls for three different types of cheeses, plenty of pork, a nice helping of fresh veggies (you may vary these, if you wish), and Ritz cracker crumb filler to give the mac 'n cheese some body and crunch. It's a great lunch or dinner side or main dish, and it makes for great leftovers, so feel free to double up on the ingredients and put one panful away in the fridge or freezer for a later date.

2 tablespoons (¼ stick, 1 ounce) butter, melted	¼ cup cheddar cheese
¼ cup smoked ham, chopped	¼ cup Gruyère or Swiss cheese
¼ cup bacon, cooked and chopped	¼ cup peas
¼ cup mushrooms, sliced	¾ pound farfalle or fusilli pasta, cooked al dente
¼ cup tomato, chopped	6 Ritz crackers, crushed
¾ cup heavy cream	Salt and pepper to taste
¼ cup Gouda cheese	

1. Preheat the oven to 350°F. In a large saucepan, melt the butter and warm the ham and bacon lightly for about 2 minutes. Add the mushrooms and tomato. Cook till limp and the liquid has released, another 3 minutes or so.

2. Add the heavy cream, Gouda, cheddar, and Gruyère or Swiss cheeses, and the peas; turn the heat to low. Allow to simmer for about 3–6 minutes or until reduced by half until the mixture is thick enough to coat the back of a spoon. Add the cooked pasta and stir until fully coated. Season with salt and pepper to taste. Blend in the Ritz cracker crumbs and bake in the oven for about 10 minutes or until golden brown on top. Serves 4.

LAMB BURGERS WITH CILANTRO AND GOAT CHEESE

A1 DINER, GARDINER, ME

You may want to do these burgers on your outdoor grill, in a cast-iron skillet, or even on a stovetop or plug-in griddle. Whichever method you choose, these lamb burgers have a distinctively Mediterranean flavor, and you can serve them with or without a bun. No mint sauce or other condiments are really needed for these tasty burgers—they're fine on their own.

2	pounds ground lamb
4	cloves fresh garlic, minced
1	teaspoon dry mustard
½	cup fresh cilantro, minced
¾	teaspoon salt
¾	teaspoon pepper
1	8-ounce package goat cheese (any kind will do)

Mix all ingredients except the goat cheese in a bowl. Shape into 6–8 burger patties. In the center of each one, place a portion of goat cheese. Reform the patties to envelope the cheese within. Grill or fry the lamb patties over medium-high heat for 3–5 minutes per side for medium-rare to medium-well burgers. Serves 6.

A Rock 'n' Roll Diner with Gourmet Cuisine

665 West Main Road
Middletown, RI 02492

401-848-9500

www.blueplatedinerri.com

The 1950s retro touches are plentiful and tastefully done at the Blue Plate.

Blue Plate Diner owner Ted Karousos.

Blue Plate Diner

Newport, Rhode Island, has a pretty amazing dining scene, with its numerous high-end restaurants and quaint little cafés and bistros. Just over the border to the north and east, however, is a burgeoning culinary landscape with a wide variety of restaurants that are almost always more accessible and affordable.

One of these northeast-of-the-border eateries is the Blue Plate Diner, a massive, 4,000-square-foot restaurant, bar, and malt shop done up in a classic 1950s rock 'n' roll motif with juke boxes, two long counters with stools, a couple dozen padded booths, and lots of diner artwork gracing the walls. Unlike many cookie-cutter retro diners around the country, this one sets itself apart with its upscale, almost gourmet-style cooking that's all done from scratch in a large, busy, semi-exposed kitchen.

Owner Ted Karousos is a second-generation restaurateur. His father was a celebrated master chef, cooking instructor, and former president and founder of the International Institute of Culinary Arts in Fall River, Massachusetts. Under Dad's watchful eye, Ted spent a number of years working in high-end kitchens, learning the restaurant trade from the bottom up. Once he and his wife began having children, Ted sought out places to take his young brood where everyone could feel relaxed and have some great food at the same time.

This desire for great cuisine in a relaxed atmosphere inspired Ted to open the Blue Plate Diner on West Main Road in Middletown in a building that had previously housed a large Chinese restaurant. After a $1 million retrofitting (several times more money than most diners get started with) and the creation of a totally unique menu, he was ready to open his doors to the curious public in 2005.

What sets the Blue Plate apart from other diners in many ways is its unique take on diner food, ratcheting up the quality and ingredients well above what you'll find at most other diner establishments. Take, for instance, the Blue Plate's Kick'd Up Mac and Cheese (see page 128), which dresses up a diner standard with ham, bacon, mushrooms, tomatoes, and peas. Then there's the Lobster and Brie Grilled Cheese (see page 121), which takes the classic American sandwich to a completely different level of taste and enjoyment. And don't miss their Signature Meat Loaf Marsala. They take a hefty slice of meat loaf, dredge it in peppercorns, pan sear it, then top it with a sweet marsala and mushroom wine gravy.

There are also a number of upscale seasonal dishes at the Blue Plate that are matched perfectly to each time of year. Autumn features Pumpkin Pancakes with Caramelized Bananas, Pecans, and Raisins (see page 26); and Butternut Squash Soup with Maple Crème Fraîche, Blue Cheese, and Cranberry (see page 52). On cold winter days, treat yourself to some Roast Turkey with Sausage Stuffing (see page 80) and a serving of warm, sweet Chocolate Bread Pudding with Rum–Brown Sugar Glaze (see page 171). Spring brings Easter and Greek Roast Leg of Lamb with Mint Pesto (see page 137), while summer features such seafood specialties as Lobster Corn Fritters with Citrus Aioli (see page 156).

If all this sounds a little too fancy-pants, worry not, for there are plenty of straightforward diner meals, sandwiches, and sides to choose from on the Blue Plate's standard menu. Eggs, pancakes, French toast, and waffles may be had any time of day, as well as omelets, other egg dishes, and standard diner sides like corned beef hash, Canadian bacon, and chouriço sausage. There are five different types of Ruebens on the sandwich menu, as well as a dozen different types of burgers—and, once again wandering a bit into the exotic, the Blue Plate's famous

The Blue Plate's broad, eclectic menu has something for everyone.

Portobello Mushroom Fries served with a cup of ranch dressing on the side.

The Blue Plate is one of those rare diners with a fully stocked bar that lines one of the walls on the backside of the dining room. There are some 20 chrome stools facing it, where you can order your favorite libation (not just beer or wine) and grab a meal at the same time. There are also about a dozen different specialty milk shakes, such as Mom's Apple Pie (it really *does* taste like apple pie; see page 169), the Black Forest Shake (think chocolate), and for the truly adventurous, there's the Chocolate Peanut Butter Banana Shake, which sort of gives you breakfast, lunch, and dessert all at the same time.

Ted Karousos has created a uniquely wonderful diner experience that was inspired by his growing family—a place where kids can be kids and where adults can have some good food (and a nerve-settling cocktail or two, if desired). This place is a must-stop for any family visiting the Newport area. Check it out.

SWEET AND SPICY STEAK TACOS WITH CHIMICHURRI SAUCE

Though it's nearly 2,000 miles from the Texas–Mexico border, the Blue Plate Diner serves up some decent Tex-Mex specialties from time to time, including this sweet and spicy treat that features rubbed flank steak thinly sliced and served on warm flour tortillas with shredded cabbage, a special sauce, and a spicy, homemade salsa.

BLUE PLATE SPICE RUB

- ½ cup sugar
- 2 tablespoons salt
- 2 tablespoons garlic powder
- ½ cup cumin
- 2 tablespoons black pepper
- 2 tablespoons paprika
- 1 tablespoon cayenne

TOMATO-JALAPEÑO PICO DE GALLO SALSA

- ½ Spanish onion
- 6 tomatoes, chopped and seeded
- 2 jalapeño peppers, seeded and finely chopped
- Juice of 2 limes
- Salt to taste

CHIMICHURRI SAUCE

- 1 cup fresh parsley, chopped
- 1 cup fresh cilantro, chopped
- ¾ cup canola oil
- 3 tablespoons white vinegar
- 2 jalapeño peppers, seeded and chopped
- 2 tablespoons dry oregano
- 4 teaspoons ground cumin
- 1 teaspoon salt
- ½ cup fresh garlic, minced
- Dash of crushed red pepper flakes

TACOS

- 5 pounds flank steak, trimmed
- 6 tablespoons honey mustard dressing
- Shredded cabbage
- Flour tortillas

1. To make the Blue Plate spice rub, tomato-jalapeño pico de gallo salsa, and chimichurri sauce, blend each recipe's ingredients together in separate bowls. Refrigerate the salsa for 1 hour before serving.

2. To prepare the flank steak, coat it with the honey mustard dressing, then rub it liberally with the Blue Plate spice rub. Cover and refrigerate for at least 1 hour.

3. On a hot grill, cook the flank steak to desired doneness, 12 minutes total for medium rare (recommended). Let rest for 10–15 minutes, then slice on the bias into thin strips.

4. Assemble the tacos by placing crunchy shredded cabbage in the center of each open-faced flour tortilla. Top with flank steak, salsa, and chimichurri sauce. Serves 10–12.

The Two Sides of 4 Aces Diner

✕ 23 Bridge Street
West Lebanon, NH 03784

☎ 603-298-5515

ⓘ www.4acesdiner.com

4 Aces Diner

About one-third of the way up the New Hampshire–Vermont border in the town of West Lebanon, New Hampshire, sits the 4 Aces Diner. It's on US 4 (Bridge Street), overlooking a temporary bridge spanning the Connecticut River to the west. It's initially hard to discern that 4 Aces is in fact a diner until you take a closer look. There's a 1952 Worcester diner car that's pretty much intact and that constitutes much of the building's ground floor. However, a red, house-like clapboard wood structure has been built over the top and down the sides of the diner car, giving it a sort of camouflage. The wooden exoskeleton provides extra seating, kitchen, storage, and office space, but it's the old diner car that takes center stage here.

The 4 Aces leads two lives—one is the weekday existence of just about any old-fashioned diner, and the other is a bacchanalia of gourmet diner-type food for the weekend crowd that comes down from nearby Dartmouth College. It's interesting to compare the two menus: Monday through Friday features slightly upscale diner offerings, such as Irish and Mexican breakfast dishes, various innovative eggs Benedict plates, hand-formed Angus beef burgers, and a variety of hot lunch platters.

Elvis is still in the building at 4 Aces.

Come Saturday and Sunday, things get fancier with such offerings as Pan-Seared Tuna Cake Eggs Benedict with sesame and ginger and a wasabi hollandaise sauce. Or you might try the Grilled Shrimp and Strawberry Salad, which comes in a sun-dried tomato tortilla bowl filled with exotic greens. Four Aces also makes its own doughnuts daily, and on the weekends they feature a maple-glazed sour cream doughnut that's split in half, tossed on the grill, and served with hot maple syrup and whipped cream.

Sibling co-owners Steve Shorey and Leann Briggs keep it light and fun throughout the week, and the decor inside the diner is as whimsical as it is nostalgic. Many of the diner car's original features are still intact, such as the floor tiles, the stainless steel backsplashes, and the recessed lighting along the ceiling lines. There are also several bright red, umbrellaed picnic tables out back where there are outdoor grills serving up seasonal barbecue specialties.

4 Aces is the diner of choice when visiting the Lebanon/White River Junction area of New Hampshire and Vermont. It's built with a lot of love, even if it's a bit hard to find beneath that red clapboard building wrapped around it.

Hiding beneath a red clapboard building is the 4 Aces Worcester-style dining car.

AMERICAN CHOP SUEY

RED ARROW DINER, MANCHESTER, NH

Chop suey is a bit of a misnomer for this dish from New Hampshire's best-known and most popular diner. When you close your eyes and take a forkful of this chop suey, dream not of floating down the Yangtze River but of punting on the canals of Venice. This dish has a strong Italian influence, and the oregano, basil, garlic, and tomato sauce drive that point home decisively. It's a classic New England diner dish that's a workingman's favorite.

2	pounds ground beef		½	tablespoon fresh garlic, chopped
1	cup onions, diced		1	tablespoon freshly ground black pepper
1	cup green bell peppers, diced		1	29-ounce can diced tomatoes
½	tablespoon granulated garlic		1	32-ounce jar pasta sauce
½	tablespoon oregano		3	cups tomato sauce
½	tablespoon basil		1	6-ounce can tomato paste
½	tablespoon Flavor-Glow		2	pounds dry macaroni noodles

In a large pot, sauté the first nine ingredients listed above together, until tender. Add the diced tomatoes, pasta sauce, tomato sauce, and tomato paste and cook until steaming and bubbling, then turn the heat down to a simmer. Cook the macaroni in boiling water until al dente, strain, add to the sauce, and mix well. Serves 12.

GREEK ROAST LEG OF LAMB WITH MINT PESTO

BLUE PLATE DINER, MIDDLETOWN, RI

Numerous diners throughout New England (and the entire East Coast, for that matter) are owned and run by Greek Americans and their families. Many of them feature such standard Greek dishes at pastitsio, gyros, and moussaka, as well as desserts such as baklava and galaktoboureko.

Spring brings Easter, and Easter is best celebrated in the Greek-American tradition with roast leg of lamb. It's a relatively simple roasted dish to prepare, especially in the scaled-down Mediterranean style, which wisely practices the credo of keeping it simple and healthy. This is a fine Greek leg of lamb recipe that may be served with an unusual and zesty mint pesto sauce.

MINT PESTO

- 4 sprigs of fresh mint
- Juice of half a lemon
- 4 tablespoons fresh garlic, minced
- 1 cup extra virgin olive oil
- 6 tablespoons Parmesan cheese
- 4 tablespoons mint jelly

LAMB

- 1 leg of spring lamb (5 pounds boneless; rolled, and tied; best procured from the butcher)
- 4 cloves fresh garlic, peeled and sliced
- Salt and black pepper to taste

1. To make the mint pesto, in a food processor, combine the mint, lemon, and garlic. Pulse lightly for 4–6 seconds. Slowly add the olive oil and Parmesan cheese and pulse until smooth. Add the mint jelly and continue to pulse.

2. To prepare the lamb, preheat the oven to 350°F. Cut slits in the top of the leg of lamb every 4 inches or so, deep enough to push the slices of garlic into the meat under the fat cap. Salt and pepper the leg liberally.

3. Roast the lamb in a roasting pan in the oven until cooked medium well (with an internal temperature of 160°F), 45–60 minutes. It should only have a slight pink color. Remove from the oven and let rest for at least 10–15 minutes before carving, then top slices with the mint pesto. Serves 12.

Diner Sides

One of the nicest things about diner food is the many side dishes that add so much culinary color to the diner experience. Corned beef hash, homefries, crispy hash browns, cole slaw, French fries, baked beans, fritters, onion rings, and potato salad are just a sampling of what's served up to complement breakfasts, sandwiches, and dinner platters at diners throughout New England. Sometimes side orders can be the highlight of any diner meal.

Hash is probably the side dish most synonymous with diners, which are frequently nicknamed "hash houses," especially if their hash is of unusual or superior quality. This chapter features three very different hash types—Corned Beef Hash from O'Rourke's, Red Flannel Hash from the Maine Diner, and Clam Hash from a now defunct roadhouse restaurant in Connecticut. Each recipe is redolent of New England charm and contains ingredients and flavors that aptly characterize the region.

Homefries, or American fries, as they're also called, often occupy a warm corner of a diner's griddle, ready to be seasoned and heated up on a moment's notice. There are a couple of recipes here for Homefries, as well as a more upscale one for smaller, more tender fingerling potatoes.

The two fritter recipes call for different types of seafood—clams for one, lobster for the other. They also require a certain amount of deep frying in order to be cooked properly. So, stock up on some high-quality vegetable oil and pull out the fryolater or cast-iron skillet and prepare to get a little messy.

In a nod to Quebec there's a great recipe for the French Canadian dish known as Poutine, which calls for potatoes, a rich beef gravy, and cheddar cheese curds. This may be converted into a main dish simply by upping the quantity. Bon appetite!

CORNED BEEF HASH

O'ROURKE'S DINER, MIDDLETOWN, CT

Corned beef hash is a diner staple, and a number of diners stake their reputations on the dish. This version, from the famed O'Rourke's Diner, comes out best when cooked on a griddle, but a good cast-iron skillet or other heavy frying pan will work just as well. Be sure to check out the recipe for O'Rourke's Dubliner Omelet (see page 15), for which this corned beef hash acts as a tasty omelet filling.

4	cups cooked corned beef, finely chopped
1½	cups cooked potatoes, finely chopped
3	eggs
1	teaspoon celery seed
1	teaspoon Cajun seasoning
1	teaspoon dry mustard (preferably Coleman's)
½	cup ketchup

To finely chop the corned beef and potatoes, grind them together in a food processor. Pulse until the mixture has some texture, but make sure it doesn't turn into baby food. Transfer the mixture to a bowl, add the remaining ingredients, and mix by hand until everything comes together. Form into patties, and brown on both sides in an oiled frying pan or on a griddle. Serves 6.

HOMEFRIES

PALACE DINER, BIDDEFORD, ME

Good homefries are always the hallmark of a quality diner. The homefried potatoes served up at the Palace Diner are superb, and now you can make them at home with this simple recipe. Feel free to use your imagination with the seasonings. It's pretty much anything goes, and some of the Palace's favorites are listed here.

2–3	pounds red potatoes, diced into 1-inch cubes
¼	cup (½ stick, 2 ounces) salted butter
	Seasonings (salt, pepper, Lowry's seasoned salt, onion powder, and garlic powder work well in any combination)

1. Preheat the oven to 450°F. You can peel the potatoes before dicing, if you wish, but the skins add flavor and texture. Rinse the cubed potatoes in cold water. Boil them in a pot until a fork can penetrate, but no longer, then remove them immediately from the hot water.

2. Toss the still-warm potatoes with the butter and the seasonings of your choice in a large bowl until the potatoes are thoroughly coated. Bake the potatoes on cookie sheets or other baking sheets for 30–40 minutes until golden brown and crispy. Serves 6.

POUTINE

PALACE DINER, BIDDEFORD, ME

Poutine is to Canadian greasy spoons and diners what hash browns and homefries are to their American counterparts—a warm, filling potato dish—with a ladleful of gravy and some cheese curds thrown in for good measure. The old mill town of Biddeford, Maine, has long been home to a sizable community of French Canadian expats, and Biddeford's Palace Diner makes them feel right at home with their version of the Canadian mainstay. This may seem like quite a bit of work for what seems on the surface to be a fairly pedestrian potato dish, but you'll be amazed at how flavorful and satisfying it is, either as a side or a main dish.

BEEF GRAVY

- 1 cup (2 sticks, 8 ounces) butter
- 2 tablespoons beef base (preferably Better Than Bouillon)
- ¼ cup all-purpose flour
- 4 cups half-and-half
- 1 rounded tablespoon freshly ground black pepper
- 1 teaspoon salt
- 3 tablespoons Gravy Master

POUTINE

- Homefries (see pages 141, 152)
- 1 cup (2 sticks, 8 ounces) butter, divided
- 5 cups cheddar cheese curds
- 5 cups gravy

1. To make the beef gravy, melt the butter in a pot over medium heat. Add the bouillon to the melted butter. Whisk until blended. Slowly add the flour, whisking until the mixture is thickened. Then slowly add the half-and-half, whisking constantly. Add the salt and pepper, the Gravy Master, and bring all to a boil, still stirring with a whisk. Turn off the heat when the gravy starts to boil. Pour into a cool pot or bowl and set aside.

2. To prepare the poutine, for each serving, grill and crush ½ pound of homefries in butter on a griddle or skillet. Cook until hot. Top with ½ cup of cheese curds. Cover and melt curds into the potatoes. Put each serving into a bowl and top with ½ cup of warm beef gravy. Serves 10.

Poutine, right; corned beef hash, left.

Pass the Poutine, S'il Vous Plaît

🍴 18 Franklin Street
Biddeford, ME

☎ 207-284-0015

ⓘ www.palacedinerme.com

This signage on the diner's front is definitely old-school original.

Palace Diner

The Palace Diner, reputed to be Maine's oldest, sits hidden in seemingly plain view on a backstreet in downtown Biddeford. This 1927 Pollard original dining car from Lowell, Massachusetts, is a classic, as you'll see once you find it tucked behind one of the stately brick buildings on Main Street. Its red and black color scheme with gold lettering on the front looks great any time of year and especially in autumn, when the surrounding foliage is in full splendor.

The Palace has been owned by several different families over the years. First, it was Louis LaChance and his clan serving up diner fare to many of his fellow French Canadian transplants, who populated Biddeford when its mills and factories were in their heyday. One of the most popular dishes served at the Palace over the years has been Poutine (see page 142), a French Canadian specialty consisting of grilled homefries and melted cheddar cheese curds smothered in homemade beef gravy.

Beginning in the 1960s, three other families in succession owned the diner until David Capotosto and his family took possession of the Palace in 2011, restored it to its near original appearance, and upgraded the kitchen. Dave's wife, Carmel, their three children, and son-in-law handled the lion's share of chores around the Palace, making it truly a family affair.

They kept intact the small, intimate scale of the diner. It has 15 stools along the counter and no booths or other seating, the same as it has been ever since the diner opened in the 1920s.

The Capotostos closed the diner in the fall of 2013, but it will reopen under new ownership in 2014. If you happen to be in Biddeford, take a drive by and check out the diner's lovely exterior. Who knows, if the lights are on inside and there are customers seated on the stools and hunched over the counter, you may be in the right place at the right time to experience the next chapter in this classic diner's storied life.

MAINE'S
OLDEST DINER
PALACE
DINER

RED FLANNEL HASH

MAINE DINER, WELLS, ME

Red flannel hash is a New England tradition going back more than a hundred years. What makes it red? Beets, of course! Before you turn your nose up at this unusual dish, give it a try—even if you think you hate beets, you'll be pleasantly surprised. And, unlike many red flannel hash recipes that use bacon, this classic rendition from the Maine Diner calls for good, old-fashioned corned beef. The Maine Diner only makes red flannel hash on Saturdays—and they make it from their New England Boiled Dinner (see page 85), which is served on Thursdays.

1½ cups cooked corned beef, finely chopped

1½ cups boiled potatoes, finely chopped

1½ cups boiled beets, chopped (canned beets are fine)

1 onion, minced

1 teaspoon Worcestershire sauce

2 tablespoons (¼ stick, 1 ounce) butter

Salt and freshly ground pepper to taste

In a large bowl, mix together the corned beef, potatoes, beets, onion, Worcestershire sauce, and salt and pepper to taste. Heat the butter in a skillet and add the meat mixture. Cook over low heat until thoroughly hot. Continue to cook until browned and nicely crusted underneath. Serves 6.

CLAM CAKES

EVELYN'S DRIVE IN, TIVERTON, RI

These tasty, deep-fried, clam-inflected morsels are a Rhode Island tradition, dating back to the early 1900s when clam cakes were supposedly invented at Aunt Carrie's seafood shack on the other side of Narragansett Bay in western Rhode Island. Clam cakes go great with a steaming cup or bowl of chowder or as a snack or a side and served with some tartar sauce.

4	cups vegetable oil
1	pound fritter mix (preferably Drum Rock, available online)
1	8-ounce can of minced clams (sea clams are preferred)
½	cup warm water

1. Carefully heat the vegetable oil in a heavy pot or high-lipped skillet to 350°F. Blend the fritter mix with the minced clams and the juice from the can. Slowly mix in the warm water until you have a sticky, smooth mixture.

2. With an ice cream scooper or a tablespoon, scoop dollops of the clam/fritter mixture and form into ball shapes. Carefully place the fritter balls in the hot oil (be careful not to splatter the hot oil) and cook for 5 minutes, turning the fritters once or twice. Drain the fritters on paper towels and serve with tartar sauce or clam chowder. Makes 10–15 clam cakes.

"Make Mine All Around!"

✕ 36 South Street
   Natick, MA 01760

ⓘ www.caseysdiner.com

Casey's famous ten-stool counter.

Casey's Diner

Casey's Diner in the western Boston suburb of Natick is one of the old-est and smallest diners in existence. The pint-size building was manu-factured by the Worcester Lunch Car Company in 1922. It has 10 stools and no tables and measures a mere 20 feet from one end of the counter to the other and 10 feet from the front door to the back wall. (There's a small building attached to the back of the diner, which is used primar-ily for storage.)

Don't be fooled, however, by the diner's diminutive size. Casey's has been packing customers in ever since Fred Casey bought the building and moved it from neighboring Framingham to Natick in 1927. Current owner Patrick Casey is the fourth generation of the Casey family to be running the place, and its popularity among locals and out-of-towners hasn't diminished over the years. All Casey has to do is show up on any given day and unlock the pocket doors on the front and side of the diner, and the customers start pouring in.

What makes this place such a stalwart and so popular to genera-tions of loyal and dedicated customers? One word (actually, two): *hot dogs*. About the only thing served at Casey's is their famous steamed hot dogs that "snap" when you bite into them, due to their natural casing. And about the only way to have a hot dog at Casey's is to have it "all around"—served on a steamed bun that's lined with yellow mustard, green pickle relish, and finely chopped raw onion before the freshly steamed wiener is placed inside. (You can also get ketchup slathered on, if you wish.) There are a few other items on the menu, such as burg-ers, a limited number of sandwiches, and a Friday fish fry special, but it would be a culinary crime to patronize Casey's and not have a hot dog.

The wieners sit in a pot of steaming water behind the counter, right next to an antique-looking copper box that houses the steamed buns. Patrick mans the hot dog operation, with a fork in one hand to extract

Casey's Diner has been a fixture in Natick, Massachusetts, since 1927.

The diner's interior is classic, with original tile work on the floor, oak trim throughout, and spindly stools with small seats that were clearly designed for a more slender, Depression-era crowd. In addition to the wiener works, there's an ancient, gas-fired griddle where burgers and grilled cheese sandwiches are made. An equally ancient coffee urn and a small sandwich prep area are the only other accouterments that Casey needs to run his operation.

It should come as no surprise that Casey's is listed on the National Register of Historic Places. It's a gem of a building and also a gem of an eatery that harkens back to the days when hard-working people could stop in, grab a cup of coffee and a quick bite to eat, and hit the road on their way to work or back home. Quick food, good prices, and friendly service have been hallmarks of Casey's Diner for decades. Natick wouldn't be the same without it.

wieners from the water and a bun in the other. There's a very busy order window on the side of the diner next to the wiener setup, so Casey doesn't have to travel far between taking orders from the window or counter and preparing the hot dogs. He holds court with those sitting near him at the counter and those outside the window. He opines about anything related to Boston sports and politics, as well as many other topics. He's a local legend, as his father, grandfather, and great-grandfather were before him, and people stop by just to see him as frequently as they do to have one of his famous tube steaks.

The diner's old-fashioned hot dog and bun steamers.

FINGERLINGS

O'ROURKE'S DINER, MIDDLETOWN, CT

The most common potato sides at diners are homefries, hash browns, and French fries. At O'Rourke's, tiny, tender fingerling potatoes are also on the potato roster. These tender, versatile tubers are an excellent side dish, and they're easy to prepare, with just a little boiling, seasoning, and pan frying. Though they're a bit pricier than most other potatoes, they're well worth the extra cost. Brian O'Rourke recommends procuring fingerlings of roughly equal size, which will cook up more uniformly.

2	pounds fingerling potatoes
2	tablespoons salt
2	tablespoons shortening (use bacon grease when possible for added flavor)
1	onion, diced
	Cajun seasoning to taste

1. Rinse the potatoes, place them in a pot, and cover them with cold water. Add 2 tablespoons of salt, bring to a boil for 2 minutes, and turn off the heat. Check the potatoes with a fork every 2–3 minutes until they're cooked through. If you have different-size potatoes, remove the smaller ones as they get done. Drain the potatoes, slicing the larger ones in half.

2. Heat the shortening in a pan, then add the onions and potatoes. When the potatoes have browned, toss the mixture with Cajun seasoning. Serves 6–8.

The Broil King Professional Griddle

Much of the best food at diners comes off griddles—usually professional-grade ones that have several square feet of surface area and a trough for the griddle cook to scrape excess cooking oil, grease, and bits of food into. A consistent, evenly heated griddle is the secret to perfect pancakes, bacon, sausage, hash browns, homefries, grilled cheese sandwiches, burgers, and so much more.

Is it possible to replicate the griddle experience at home? The short answer is yes, and the griddle of choice, according to America's Test Kitchen and a few other independent reviewers, is the Broil King Professional Griddle. It's big enough to hold eight pancakes or 1 pound of bacon at a time, it has a foolproof grease-draining system, and most important, it heats quickly, evenly, and consistently. It even has stainless steel back and side splashes, which are both practical and aesthetically pleasing to diner aficionados.

The Broil King Professional Griddle will set you back about $125 to $150, but if you want to master the art of true diner cookery and your household can withstand a constant barrage of griddle-cooked food, then there's no better choice. There's even a commercial-grade countertop version that sells for around $500. You can check them out at www.broilking.com/griddle.

Give one of these griddles a try in your kitchen, then start shopping around for an old diner to restore, open your own eatery, and start living the dream!

HOMEFRIES

MAINE DINER, WELLS, ME

You can often judge a diner by the quality of its fried potatoes. The Maine Diner does an excellent job, and you can, too, by following this quick and simple recipe for foolproof homefries that go great with virtually any meal, especially breakfast.

2	pounds red bliss potatoes
2	tablespoons canola oil
1	tablespoon fresh parsley, chopped
1	teaspoon garlic powder
	Salt and pepper to taste

1. Preheat the oven to 450°F. Boil the potatoes until they are easily pierced with a fork, and drain well. Chop the potatoes into 1-inch cubes.

2. Spread the oil in the bottom of a 9 x 12-inch baking dish. Put the cubed potatoes in the pan; sprinkle with the parsley, garlic powder, and salt and pepper to taste; and bake for 12–15 minutes, until the potatoes are golden brown. Serves 6–8.

CLAM HASH

This recipe is based on a recipe from Roadfood.com, the website of *Roadfood* co-authors Jane and Michael Stern. It's derived from a clam hash recipe that was used at Pat's Kountry Kitchen, a recently closed Connecticut eatery. Pat Kline claims she came up with the recipe when her kids threw away some broth from a batch of recently cooked clams, which meant there wouldn't be any clam chowder at the restaurant that day. Ever resourceful, Pat minced the clams and blended them into her standard hash recipe, and voilà, clam hash. Roadfood.com says this version hues closely to Pat's original.

3	medium potatoes (about 1 pound)	2–4	tablespoons cream
1	dozen chowder clams or two 6½-ounce cans chopped or minced clams, mostly drained		Salt to taste
1	rib celery, diced	½	teaspoon black pepper
½	bay leaf, crumbled	¼	teaspoon thyme
2	bunches scallions, chopped (including a bit of the green parts)	⅛–¼	pound salt pork, cut into small pieces

1. Peel and boil the potatoes in a pot until they can be pierced with a fork. Cool and dice. Scrub the clam shells thoroughly clean under cold water. Place them in a large pot with about an inch of water and add the celery and crumbled bay leaf. Cover and steam over medium heat about 15 minutes or until the shells have popped wide open.

2. Remove the clams from the broth. When they're cool enough to handle, scoop out the clam meat and chop fine. (If you go the canned-clam route, you may skip the steaming step along with the celery and bay leaf.)

3. Combine the chopped clams, potatoes, and scallions in a bowl. Add the cream and stir until the mixture holds together like a lumpy paste, but isn't set. Blend in the seasonings using a spoon.

4. In a heavy skillet, fry the chopped salt pork over medium-high heat until the fat is rendered. Remove most of the pork bits and set them aside. Spoon the hash into the skillet and flatten into a patty shape. Fry each side for 10–15 minutes until crusty and brown. Serves 3–4.

A Little Bit of Lebanon in Litchfield County

✕ 55 West Main Street
North Canaan, CT 06018

☎ 860-824-7040

ⓘ www.collinsdiner.com

Collin's Diner

Way up in the northwest corner of Connecticut, just south of the border with Massachusetts and the Berkshires, sits the pretty little town of North Canaan (not to be confused with its uber-wealthy downstate cousin, New Canaan). Just off North Canaan's main street and across the tracks from the town's historic train station you'll find a bona fide national landmark tucked into a nondescript parking lot, partially obscured by a small berm and some shrubbery. There's a diamond in the rough in northwest Litchfield County in the form of a diner that's well worth checking out.

The Collin's Diner, an original 1941 Jerry O'Mahony–manufactured diner in the streamline moderne style, has resided in North Canaan for more than 70 years. Purchased by the Lebanese husband-and-wife team of Mike and Aida Hamzy in 1969, the diner has remained in the same family ever since. The building is in the National Register of Historic Places.

The Hamzys stuck to the Collin's traditional diner-fare menu of meat loaf, burgers, pancakes, eggs, and bacon, and they eventually added some dishes that reflect their Lebanese ancestry. Management of the diner has recently passed to the Hamzys' son and daughter, Ameen-Storm and Bader, who carry on the family's tradition of basic diner cooking with Middle Eastern touches around the edges. If you happen to make it up to the Collin's and you're looking for something different to eat, try the Mjedera, a lentil paste

The Collin's Diner is a classic Jerry O'Mahoney diner manufactured in the early 1940s.

with caramelized onions served with pita bread, or the Loobi, a salad of cold sautéed string beans with onions, garlic, and roasted tomatoes.

Best of all, soak up the atmosphere of this classic rail-car-style diner, with its original wood, chrome, and tile trim inside and its glass, stainless steel, and neon exterior. This place is a favorite with nostalgia buffs and politicians, so don't be surprised if during your visit there is a sea of vintage cars or polished-up Harleys filling the parking lot, or a local, state, or even national politician seated at a booth and holding court with the locals. One can only hope that the Collin's Diner can keep it going for many years to come.

LOBSTER CORN FRITTERS WITH CITRUS AIOLI

BLUE PLATE DINER, MIDDLETOWN, RI

Clam fritters are what you normally find at seafood shacks and restaurants (and certain diners) in New England, especially in summertime. They contain bits of clam and light seasonings mixed into the dough before frying and are served with tartar sauce or a cup of chowder on the side. This more upscale version from the Blue Plate Diner calls for lobster meat and a complex mixture of flour, baking powders, buttermilk, and chopped vegetables, resulting in fritters with a little bit of everything in them. Garnish with a citrusy aioli for dipping, and you have a gourmet appetizer that's fit for an upscale diner or even a snappy Mediterranean bistro.

CITRUS AIOLI

Juice of ½ lemon

Juice of ½ lime

Juice of ½ orange

1 teaspoon fresh garlic, finely chopped

1 cup mayonnaise

1 teaspoon ground cumin

Salt and pepper to taste

LOBSTER CORN FRITTERS

1 cup all-purpose flour

½ teaspoon baking powder

½ teaspoon baking soda

½ teaspoon salt

Freshly ground black pepper

¾ cup buttermilk

1 large egg, separated

1 tablespoon (⅛ stick, ½ ounce) unsalted butter, melted

1 whole 1½-pound lobster, boiled, shelled, and chilled

¾ cup corn kernels, frozen or from the cob

4 tablespoons red onion, finely chopped

2 tablespoons green pepper, finely chopped

Cooking oil

1. To make the citrus aioli, whisk all ingredients together in a small bowl. Keep refrigerated.

2. To make the lobster corn fritters, in a large bowl, whisk together the flour, baking powder, baking soda, salt, and pepper. Set aside.

3. In a separate bowl, whisk together the buttermilk, egg yolk, and butter. Make a well in the center of the dry ingredients and pour in the buttermilk mixture. Stir lightly; then fold in the lobster, corn, red onion, and green pepper.

4. In a medium bowl, whisk the egg white into soft peaks and fold it into the batter. Let the mixture rest in the refrigerator for 1 hour.

5. In a Fryolator or heavy pan, heat 1 inch of cooking oil to 350°F. Drop four or five golf-ball-size dollops of batter into the hot oil. Cook until golden brown, about 4 minutes. Check by poking with a toothpick so that it comes out clean from the fritter. Cook the remaining batter in the same manner. Serve with citrus aioli spooned over the top or on the side. Serves 6–8.

Diner Desserts

Diners have produced some amazing desserts over the years, from puddings to cakes to crisps and ice cream delights. This chapter contains a variety of dessert recipes, some of them quite basic, along with a few that are downright complex and involved.

The three bread pudding recipes represent widely varying takes on this thick, gooey, and sweet dessert. One calls for melted toffee on top, another is crowned with a rum–brown sugar glaze, and the third comes unadorned.

Indian pudding is a classic New England dessert, and there are two recipes to choose from here. The first comes from the Maine Diner, and it's seasoned with ginger, cinnamon, and nutmeg—all three classic New England spices acquired from the seafaring days of yore. The second outlines how they make Indian pudding at Sonny's Blue Benn Diner in Vermont: allspice and blackstrap molasses are the standout ingredients in their version.

If not actually invented in New England (a debate has raged for years), whoopie pies are still wildly popular in the region, and there are two versions to choose from—one coming from the relative upstart Becky's Diner in Portland, Maine, and the other from the venerable Moody's Diner some 100 miles further up the coast. Again, compare and contrast and give one of them a try.

In all, there are 16 desserts to explore, which is about the average number of dessert offerings at most diners in New England. Enjoy the variety—and prepare yourself for the pies and cakes that come in the next chapter.

TOFFEE BREAD PUDDING

A1 DINER, GARDINER, ME

This bread pudding comes with a nice toffee topping on it. The double-boiler-type cooking method ensures that the pudding portion won't dry out during the cooking process. It's a bit of work but well worth it.

4	eggs
¾	cup sugar
2	cups heavy cream
2½	cups half-and-half
1	teaspoon vanilla extract
6	cups soft or stale white bread, cubed
1	bag toffee chunks (with or without chocolate; either is fine)

1. Preheat the oven to 350°F. Grease a 9 x 13-inch baking pan. Mix the eggs with the sugar in a bowl large enough to hold all the ingredients. When thoroughly combined, add the heavy cream and half-and-half. Whisk until most of the sugar is dissolved, then add the cubed bread, pushing it under the liquid. Let this sit for 15 minutes or longer so the bread can absorb as much of the liquid as possible.

2. Pour the mixture into the prepared pan. Sprinkle the toffee chunks evenly over the top. Float the baking pan in a larger pan containing water, and give the bread pudding a hot water-type bath in the preheated oven for 35–45 minutes. When there isn't any liquid in the center as you push on the bread, remove the pan from the oven and the water bath. Cool the bread pudding to room temperature. Serves 8–12.

BECKY'S CHOCOLATE CHIP COOKIES

BECKY'S DINER, PORTLAND, ME

How about a little toffee, walnuts, and oatmeal in your chocolate chip cookies? That's the way they do it at Becky's Diner in Portland, Maine, and it's earned a permanent spot on their dessert menu. The oatmeal does a nice job of binding up the cookie batter, and a bit of the walnuts add crunch as well as nutty flavor.

1¼	cups (2½ sticks, 12 ounces) butter	1	teaspoon baking soda
1½	cups dark brown sugar	¾	teaspoon salt
1	cup white sugar	1	teaspoon baking powder
3	eggs	2	cups walnuts, coarsely chopped
½	tablespoon vanilla extract	3	cups chocolate chips
2	cups oatmeal	1	bag toffee pieces
2	cups all-purpose flour		

1. Preheat the oven to 350°F. Mix the butter, brown sugar, and white sugar together in a mixer, then add the eggs and vanilla and mix some more. Grind the oatmeal to a fine powder in a food processor.

2. Place all ingredients in a large bowl and mix until thoroughly combined into a smooth cookie batter. Using a small scoop (so that cookies are uniform in size), drop scoops of dough onto a greased cookie sheet and bake for 25–30 minutes. Makes approximately 24 large cookies.

INDIAN PUDDING

MAINE DINER, WELLS, ME

This New England favorite consists of cornmeal, molasses, light cream, butter, brown sugar, ginger, and cinnamon. It's best served warm and topped with a scoop of vanilla ice cream. It's a wonderful companion to a cup of coffee or tea on an autumn afternoon.

- 3 cups milk
- ¾ cup molasses
- ¾ cup cornmeal
- ½ cup sugar
- ¼ teaspoon ginger
- ¼ teaspoon cinnamon
- ¼ teaspoon nutmeg
- ¼ teaspoon salt
- ½ teaspoon vanilla extract
- 2 eggs, beaten

Vanilla ice cream (optional)

In a medium-size saucepan, heat the milk and stir in the molasses. Cook slowly, stirring. Add all the remaining ingredients, except the vanilla and beaten eggs. Continue to stir and cook until the pudding starts to thicken. Add the beaten eggs. Remove the mixture from heat when it starts to bubble. Stir in the vanilla and let cool. Top with a scoop of vanilla ice cream. Serves 4–6.

LEMON LUSH

Lemon Lush is one of those Betty Crocker–type chilled desserts that are great on a hot summer day. It's sort of like lemon meringue pie, minus the showy "hairdo" on top. This version has its own fluffy, nutty top layer, and the other three layers are equally rich and impressive.

1	cup (2 sticks, 8 ounces) butter, softened
1	cup all-purpose flour
1	cup walnuts, chopped and divided
1½	cups cream cheese
3	cups confectioners' sugar
1	cup Cool Whip, divided
2	packages instant lemon pudding mix
3	cups whole milk

1. Preheat the oven to 350°F. To make the base layer, in a small bowl, mix together the butter, flour, and half the chopped walnuts. Press the mixture into the bottom of a 9 x 13-inch greased pan. Bake until golden, approximately 15–20 minutes, then set aside to cool.

2. In a medium-size bowl, combine the cream cheese, confectioners' sugar, and half the Cool Whip, and spread it over the cooled base layer.

3. In a large bowl, mix together the instant lemon pudding mix and whole milk until the mix dissolves, and spread this mixture over the second layer.

4. Top off the Lemon Lush with the remaining Cool Whip and chopped walnuts. Refrigerate for at least an hour to allow the flavors to combine before serving. Serves 9–12.

WHOOPIE PIES

Though not so much a pie as a cream-filled cake sandwich, whoopie pies have a long and colorful history in the state of Maine (and throughout New England, for that matter). This recipe is Susan Moody's original.

CREAM FILLING

2	egg whites
2	cups confectioners' sugar, divided
½	cup shortening
¼	teaspoon salt
1	teaspoon vanilla extract

PIES

¾	cup margarine
1½	cups sugar

2	eggs
½	teaspoon vanilla extract
1½	cups milk
3	cups all-purpose flour
¾	cup cocoa
¾	teaspoon baking powder
2¼	teaspoons baking soda
½	teaspoon salt

1. To make the cream filling, beat the egg whites until stiff. Add ¼ cup of the confectioners' sugar and beat. Set aside.

2. Cream together the shortening and the rest of the confectioners' sugar. Add the salt and vanilla. Stir in the egg white mixture and mix until smooth, about 2 minutes.

3. To make the pies, preheat the oven to 350°F. In a large bowl, cream together the margarine, sugar, eggs, and vanilla. Add the milk slowly and mix well.

4. In a separate bowl, combine the dry ingredients and stir into the batter. Drop the batter by the teaspoonful onto a greased cookie sheet and bake for 15 minutes. Let cool. Spread the cream filling on the pan sides of half of the cooled pie pieces, then top each one with the other half of the pie pieces. Makes approximately 20 whoopie pies.

✕ 1390 Commercial Street
Portland, ME 0410

☎ 207-773-7070

ⓘ www.beckysdiner.com

Becky's Diner

Sometimes, when a city needs a diner, the right person comes along and makes it happen. In the case of Portland, Maine, that person is Becky Rand, founder and owner of Becky's Diner. Rand opened her namesake diner after waitressing at a number of Portland eateries and coming to the realization that there was a need for comfort food down by the docks, where commercial fishermen and dockworkers arrive early in the morning and eat heartily before heading out to sea or handling cargo.

The recently divorced mother of six had to get a zoning variance in order to put her diner in an area that allowed only fishing businesses. Once that hurdle was cleared, Becky's Diner opened in 1991 as an early morning gathering place for fishermen and dockworkers. The place was hopping from the first day, and it's been busy ever since. Becky eventually added lunch and dinner hours, and the diner is now basically open from 4 am to 9 pm daily, long hours of operation by any diner standards.

Becky's is perhaps best known for super fresh seafood and killer desserts. The breakfasts, however, which are served all day, may be the most popular meals. This is not to denigrate the basic diner fare, such as the meat loaf, which is served in thick slabs smothered in beef gravy, with homemade mashed potatoes and fresh vegetables on the side. The roast turkey with sausage stuffing is made fresh daily and is so good it was featured on *Diners, Drive-Ins and Dives*.

Haddock in its various forms is the standout on the seafood side. Start with the fresh Atlantic Haddock Chowdah (that's how Becky spells it on her menu; see page 63), then move on to the broiled haddock, bathed in lemon and butter and smothered in bread crumbs. You also can't go wrong with Becky's heaping, affordably priced Fisherman's Platter with deep-fried Maine shrimp, haddock, scallops, and whole belly clams.

On the lighter side, there are fruit bowls for the morning crowd,

dinner-size salads of various types from midday onward, and broiled scallops. Kids' baskets come with side choices of fries, carrots, or applesauce. After that, it's back to the high-calorie items that one expects from a full-on diner experience, such as spaghetti and meatballs with marinara sauce, chicken parmigiana, steamed lobsters served with butter, and an array of appetizers that emanate for the most part from the deep fryers.

Becky's sign beckons along the Portland waterfront.

The building that Becky's occupies next to the waterfront is two stories tall, and much of the second story is occupied by a highly sophisticated, constantly busy baking operation. There are institutional-size baking ovens, giant refrigerators, and lots of table and counter space for rolling out the dough and assembling the baking trays. Virtually all the fresh-baked goods end up in the glass cases behind the service counter downstairs and next to the cash register by the front door. Standout dessert items include Becky's famous Blueberry Cake and Carrot Cake (see pages 194 and 202), both rich and dense in flavor and texture. The Chocolate Chip Cookies (see page 161) are augmented with walnuts and chunks of toffee, and the Whoopie Pies (see page 178) are particularly popular to-go items with kids.

The restaurant's lengthy first-floor dining room has two counters that face each other and are divided by a center-aisle service area with coffee urns and mugs, desserts on display, and soft drink dispensers. Booths line the walls on both sides of the room, providing seating for groups who don't wish to belly up to the counter. The atmosphere is always fast-paced

and convivial, especially in the early morning hours when the maritime crew is in for their first meal of the day.

Portland is in many ways the dining mecca of New England, with more restaurants per capita than anywhere else in the six-state region. Many of the city's eateries are unique, innovative, and outstanding. Among this vast array of competition, Becky's holds its own and proves it every day with packed booths and counter stools, serving good, basic diner food at reasonable prices in a friendly atmosphere. It's a family-run operation, and several of Becky's children are deeply involved in the business, so the good news is Becky's looks to be here to stay, and the fine citizens of Portland (especially the fishermen) are the primary benficiaries.

The booths at Becky's are always packed at mealtimes.

GRAPE-NUT PUDDING

EVELYN'S DRIVE-IN, TIVERTON, RI

This classic New England dessert is a favorite at Evelyn's, where it's been on the menu for many years. The cinnamon and nutmeg give it a distinctive flavor in the crowded field of pudding desserts.

5	eggs
½	cup sugar
1½	cups whole milk
1	teaspoon vanilla extract
¼	cup Grape-Nuts cereal
	Ground cinnamon
	Nutmeg
	Whipped cream or whipped topping

1. Preheat the oven to 350°F. Lightly butter an 8-inch-square baking dish. In a bowl, whisk together the eggs, sugar, milk, and vanilla extract. Pour into the baking dish. Spread the Grape-Nuts over the top, then sprinkle with cinnamon and nutmeg.

2. Place the baking dish in a larger baking dish, and add hot water to the larger dish, filling it about halfway so that the pudding dish is surrounded. Bake for 20–30 minutes until a toothpick inserted in the middle comes out clean.

3. Remove the pudding dish and let cool for at least half an hour. The pudding may be served warm or refrigerated and served chilled later on. Place a dollop of whipped cream or whipped topping on each individual serving. Serves 4–5.

MOM'S APPLE PIE MILK SHAKE

BLUE PLATE DINER, MIDDLETOWN, RI

This ice cream treat combines the warmth and comfort of apple pie with the cool refreshment of a milk shake. Once you've tried this, you may forego the baked version and stick with the shake version for your apple pie fix. The similarity in flavor is uncanny.

6 tablespoons apple pie filling or apples in syrup

4 tablespoons brown sugar

3 teaspoons cinnamon, plus more for garnish

1 graham cracker

3 scoops vanilla ice cream

½ cup whole milk

2 tablespoons whipped cream

Crumbled graham crackers for garnish

1. In a blender, combine the apple filling, brown sugar, cinnamon, graham cracker, ice cream, and milk. Blend on low for about 1 minute or until smooth and thick.

2. Pour into a 16-ounce glass and garnish with whipped cream, crumbled graham crackers, and a pinch of cinnamon. Makes 1 milk shake.

BECKY'S FUDGE BROWNIES

BECKY'S DINER, PORTLAND, ME

The chocolaty Fudge Brownies at Becky's Diner are cut into generous 3-inch squares, and you can do the same when you cook up your own batch at home.

1	cup (2 sticks, 8 ounces) butter or margarine
¾	cup unsweetened chocolate squares
3	cups sugar
1	tablespoon vanilla extract
4	eggs
1	teaspoon salt
1	teaspoon baking powder
1½	cups all-purpose flour
2	cups walnuts, chopped

Preheat the oven to 350°F. In a stainless steel saucepan, melt the butter or margarine and the chocolate squares. Remove from the heat and let cool for 5 minutes. Then add the sugar, vanilla, eggs, salt, baking powder, flour, and chopped walnuts. Stir only until mixed. Do not overmix—it dulls the baking powder and makes the brownies tough. Pour the mixture into a 9 x 13-inch buttered baking pan. Bake about 25–35 minutes, until the sides pull away from the edge of the pan. Makes approximately 12 large brownies.

CHOCOLATE BREAD PUDDING WITH RUM–BROWN SUGAR GLAZE

BLUE PLATE DINER, MIDDLETOWN, RI

Bread pudding is always a nice treat, especially in wintertime. When you add some chocolate to the mix and top it with a sweet, heady glaze of brown sugar and rum, you've got a bread pudding that won't be forgotten anytime soon!

BREAD PUDDING

- 6 eggs
- 1½ cups sugar
- 1 quart whole milk
- 1 teaspoon vanilla extract
- Dash of salt
- 1 tablespoon (⅛ stick, ½ ounce) butter, melted
- 1 loaf white bread, dry or 1-day old, diced into small cubes
- 1 bag (12 ounces) chocolate chips

RUM–BROWN SUGAR GLAZE

- ½ cup dark spiced rum
- ½ cup (1 stick, 4 ounces) whole butter
- 1 cup brown sugar

1. To make the bread pudding, preheat the oven to 300°F. In a medium-size bowl, combine the eggs and sugar; mix well and set aside.

2. In a saucepan, heat the milk, vanilla, salt, and tablespoon of butter. Bring to a light simmer; do not scald. Combine the milk mixture with the bread and the egg/sugar mixture and let it be absorbed. Add the chocolate chips.

3. Transfer the bread pudding mixture to a greased, 2-inch-deep, 9 x 13-inch baking pan. Bake for 50–60 minutes. The pudding should be slightly moist. Check by sticking a toothpick in the middle; it should come out clean.

4. To make the rum–brown sugar glaze, in a saucepan, add the rum, heat it up, and bring it to a flame for several seconds to reduce the alcohol content. On low heat, add the butter and brown sugar while stirring constantly. Do not let them separate. Pour immediately over the bread pudding. Serves 10.

A "Capitol" Idea in Downtown Lynn

✕ 431 Union Street
Lynn, MA 01901

☎ 781-595-9314

The Capitol Diner's distinctive red exterior is a joy to behold in downtown Lynn, Massachusetts.

Capitol Diner

The working class city of Lynn, Massachusetts, 10 miles northeast of Boston, has seen its fair share of ups and downs and changes over the years: the rise and fall of various industries, factory openings and closings, a shifting and changing population base, and a 2-mile-long waterfront that has become a scenic and recreational magnet.

In downtown Lynn, there's a red-and-white treasure wedged between a couple of brick buildings on Union Street: the Capitol Diner. This Brill dining car has been in place since 1928, when it was originally installed and named the Miss Lynn Diner. At one time, there

were five barber chairs in the basement for shaves and haircuts.

In 1938, new owner George Fennell renamed it the Capitol Diner, after the Capitol Theatre, which was across the street at the time. George's nephew Buddy Fennell arrived from maritime Canada in 1948 and ended up working and eventually owning the Capitol Diner during a reign that lasted more than half a century. The diner is currently under its third generation of Fennell ownership, with Buddy's son Bobby at the helm. In addition to owning and running the diner, Bobby also serves as a Massachusetts state representative for his district in Lynn. The diner is truly a family institution that maintains close ties to the neighborhood and the city.

There are a couple of unique architectural features at the Capitol Diner, in addition to the eye-catching diner car itself. First, there's a glass countertop that runs the length of the diner's interior—a feature that was more common in the heyday of diners in the early to mid-1900s. Then there's the patio and garden in front of the sideways-facing diner, where there are outdoor tables, flowers, and ornamental plantings. This little patch of green used to serve as the roaming ground for Buddy Fennell's menagerie of chickens and other small barnyard animals.

Breakfast is the busiest meal at the Capitol, and the menu is pretty straightforward, with egg and omelet dishes, corned beef hash, pancakes served unadorned or dressed up with blueberries, bananas, apples, cinnamon, or M&M's candies. A variety of grilled burgers and sandwiches dominate lunchtime offerings, along with all sorts of daily specials. In a nod to Lynn's burgeoning Latino population, there

The Capitol's glass countertop is a rarity these days in diners.

are some very nice grilled quesadillas served up at lunchtime, including chicken, steak, and vegetarian varieties.

The Fennell family has made a decades-long commitment to the city of Lynn and its people with their lovingly preserved Capitol Diner, and it's a great place to grab a quick bite to eat in a warm, friendly atmosphere with a true neighborhood diner feel to it.

BECKY'S GRAPE-NUT CUSTARD

BECKY'S DINER, PORTLAND, ME

It's quick, it's simple, it's sweet, and it's crunchy. Bake up a pan of this custard for dessert, then stand back and watch everyone come back for seconds.

6	eggs
1½	cups sugar
1	cup Grape-Nuts cereal
½	tablespoon vanilla extract
	Pinch of salt
1½	quarts whole milk

Preheat the oven to 350°F. Mix all the ingredients together and pour into a greased 9 x 13-inch cake pan. Bake for 1 hour, or until the custard is set. Serves 10.

The Worcester Lunch Car Company

Diners were in their heyday in the first half of the 1900s, and one of the most prolific builders of prefabricated diner car restaurants was the Worcester Lunch Car Company of Worcester, Massachusetts. From 1906 to 1961, the company was the leading diner builder in New England. In that stretch of 55 years, the Worcester Lunch Car Company manufactured 651 diners, and many of them found homes in cities and towns throughout the 6-state region.

There are some 90 Worcester diners still in operation in New England, and some of them have made their way onto the National Register of Historic Places. Each Worcester diner is unique, yet they share certain characteristics, such as curved, barrel-like ceilings, a resemblance to railroad cars, booths lining the windows in front, a long counter with stools, and colorful enamel exterior panels with the diner name splashed across the front. Many also have the slogan "Booth Service" next to the diner name. This was done in an attempt to lure female customers into the diners because back in the early 1900s, it was considered unladylike to sit on a stool at a counter.

Diners reached their apex after World War II, and more manufacturers got into the diner-making business, partly to sell diners to the many GIs and others who were eager to launch their own businesses. Diners were considered easy start-ups, with virtually everything supplied by the diner manufacturers.

Heading into the 1950s, Worcester Lunch Car was holding its own, but times began to change, and the company didn't adapt to restaurant owners' new demands for larger, roomier restaurants with more seating (and more profitability). The nascent fast-food industry, led by McDonald's rapid expansion across the country, also took a big bite out of the diner market. Orders for new diners began to dry up, and the company made and shipped its last diner in 1957. Sadly, the company's assets were auctioned off four years later.

Though it's been more than half a century since a true Worcester diner car rolled off the factory floor, there are still plenty of well-preserved examples that you can visit. Randy Garbin's *Diners of New England*

offers excellent descriptions of diners of every type in the region, and you can track down the Worcester diners still in existence by consulting his book. In addition, a fully restored 1926 Worcester lunch car is on display at the Culinary Arts Museum in Providence, Rhode Island; and the Henry Ford Museum in Dearborn, Michigan, is home to Lamy's Diner, an operating Worcester diner that serves food and light snacks in the midst of the magnificent automobile museum.

A photo of the first lunch car produced by the Worcester Lunch Car Company, in the early 1900s.

INDIAN PUDDING

SONNY'S BLUE BENN DINER, BENNINGTON, VT

Indian pudding is a popular regional dessert at New England diners and a variety of other establishments. This version utilizes blackstrap molasses and cornmeal, lending a new level of authenticity, even healthiness, to the dish.

1	teaspoon allspice
1	teaspoon ginger
3	cups milk
¼	cup blackstrap molasses
2	tablespoons sugar
2	tablespoons (¼ stick, 1 ounce) butter, melted
¼	teaspoon salt
	Pinch of baking powder
1	egg, beaten
1	cup yellow cornmeal

Preheat the oven to 350°F. Mix all of the ingredients together in a bowl. Pour the mixture into a lightly greased 9 x 13-inch baking pan, and bake until firm and just turning golden brown on top. Serve warm with a scoop of vanilla ice cream on each serving. Serves 5–6.

176   THE NEW ENGLAND DINER COOKBOOK

APPLE CRISP

MOODY'S DINER, WALDOBORO, ME

This recipe provides a great way to make use of the autumn apple harvest. Less tart, red-skinned apples work best, though the green varieties certainly won't disappoint.

4	cups apples, sliced
½	cup oatmeal
⅔	cup brown sugar
½	cup all-purpose flour
¾	teaspoons cinnamon
6	tablespoons (¾ stick, 3 ounces) butter or margarine, softened

Preheat the oven to 350°F. Line a greased 8 x 8-inch square pan with a ¾-inch layer of sliced apples. In a large bowl, combine the oatmeal, brown sugar, flour, and cinnamon. Cut in the butter or margarine until the mixture resembles coarse crumbs, then sprinkle it over the apple slices. Bake for 35–40 minutes. Serve warm with whipped cream on top and/or vanilla ice cream on the side. Serves 6–8.

BECKY'S WHOOPIE PIES

BECKY'S DINER, PORTLAND, ME

Whoopie pies have become a sort of summer tradition with tourists who visit Maine, but they're great to have year-round. Though there's some debate over whether whoopie pies were invented in Maine or New Hampshire or in the Amish country of southeastern Pennsylvania, there's no doubt that the tasty little cream-filled, sandwich-like "pies" are most closely associated with the Pine Tree State these days.

Becky's Diner, on the waterfront in downtown Portland, Maine, may not be the first place that comes to mind when thinking about where to go for whoopie pies, but owner Becky Rand has been serving them up to rave reviews for many years, and her recipe allows you to enjoy these treats in the comfort of your home anytime.

CREAM FILLING

- 6 egg whites
- 2¼ cups shortening
- 6 cups confectionary sugar
- ¼ teaspoon salt
- 1 tablespoon real vanilla

COOKIES

- 1 cup shortening
- 2 cups sugar
- 4 eggs
- 4 cups all-purpose flour
- 9 tablespoons cocoa
- 2 teaspoons baking powder
- 2 teaspoons baking soda
- 2 teaspoons salt
- 2 cups whole milk, plus 2 tablespoons vinegar (added as a souring agent)
- 1 tablespoon vanilla extract

1. To make the cream filling, in a medium-size bowl, beat the egg whites until stiff. Set aside. In a large bowl, mix together the shortening, sugar, salt, vanilla. Fold in the stiff egg whites and mix well.

2. To make the cookies, preheat the oven to 375°F. In a large bowl, mix together the shortening and the sugar, add the eggs, and sift the dry ingredients into the bowl. Add the sour milk and vanilla and beat well.

3. Spoon 3-inch dollops of batter onto a greased cookie sheet. Bake for 8–10 minutes, depending on the size of the dollops, until the tops are dry. Remove from the oven and cool on a rack. Spread the frosting on one cookie and top with another to form a sandwich. Makes 15–20 whoopie pies.

That Great, Green New Hampshire Diner

✕ 10 Depot Street
Peterborough, NH 03458

☎ 603-924-6202

ⓘ www.peterboroughdiner.com

Peterborough Diner

In the artsy community of Peterborough, New Hampshire, there's lots to see and do in the way of galleries, theater, music, and arts festivals. The town is home to the famed MacDowell Art Colony, which has served as a retreat for artists since the early 1900s. Thorton Wilder wrote much of his Pulitzer Prize–winning play, *Our Town,* while in residence there.

In the quaint, walkable downtown area, there are lots of shops, coffee spots, a large and well-stocked bookstore, and a deep green–colored 1950 Worcester diner car, plopped down at a rakish angle on a sliver of land at the base of a tree-covered hill. The Peterborough Diner has been in this same spot for more than 60 years, and it maintains much of the great looks and fine spirit that it had when it first opened its doors to the town's curious citizens in the early 1950s.

The best thing about the Peterborough Diner is the building itself. You take a step back in time when you enter—much of the diner's interior is the original wood, tile, and stainless steel. The griddle was removed from behind the counter and moved to a back room, where a kitchen was built around it. The original restrooms were also removed along the side of the diner and repositioned in back, which freed up space for several more tables. Diners often struggle with a lack of space for customers, which cuts into profits, but the Peterborough has ameliorated the problem with the side room addition and several nicely appointed picnic tables out front, which greatly increase seating capacity.

With 8 booths and 16 stools, the main dining car is the place to be in order to soak up the diner ambience of the place. The curved barrel ceiling of the old diner car and the ceiling fans softly whirring above create an atmosphere of warmth and intimacy.

A classic Western Omelet with all the fixings at the Peterborough.

The green façade of the Peterborough Diner blends perfectly with the verdant hills behind it.

The booths are cozy and tightly packed together, and the chrome-plated, naugahyde-padded stools put you right in front of the action occurring on the other side of the counter.

The menu reads like a primer for Diner Food 101. It's straightforward breakfast plates, lunch sandwiches, and dinner platters such as meat loaf, pot roast, and open-faced turkey or roast beef sandwiches. The Peterborough prides itself in its ice cream offerings, so try a sundae, a frappé (milk shake), or a root beer float. The prices are more than reasonable, and the portions generous—as it should be at any diner worth visiting.

It's always surprising to see rail car–style Worcester diners out in the countryside, and the Peterborough Diner is no exception. But the locals are still grateful for their bright, green diner machine, and one can only hope that its longevity continues for many years to come.

URBAN'S BUTTERNUT SQUASH

O'ROURKE'S DINER, MIDDLETOWN, CT

Brian O'Rourke is known for coming up with new dishes almost every day, and he often improvises with what he finds in the diner's larder each morning. When I showed up to get a recipe or two from him, he told me he'd be making Urban's Butternut Squash. "You know someone else named Urban?" I asked. "No," he replied. "I'm going to make it up right now, and it's named after you." Make it up he did, and the end result is this tasty squash-based dessert that's sweet and healthy at the same time.

1–2	good-size butternut squash	2–3	cardamom pods
2	cups brewed coffee	2	eggs, beaten
½	cup maple syrup	1	cup half-and-half
2–3	cups all-purpose flour	3	teaspoons vanilla extract
¼	cup confectioners' sugar	4–6	tablespoons (½–¾ stick, 2–3 ounces) butter
2	pinches of allspice	4–6	tablespoons mascarpone cheese
1	cup pistachios, shelled	1	tablespoon honey
1	cup oatmeal		Dash of lavender
1	cup panko bread crumbs		Ground cherries
1	cup sweet bread crumbs		

1. Slice the butternut squash in half, setting the bulbous gourd section aside. Peel the neck portion, using a hand peeler, firmly stroking away from your body until the outer skin is removed. Slice the peeled squash neck into ½-inch-thick round disks.

2. Warm the coffee and maple syrup in a pan and poach the gourd disks in the liquid under medium heat until tender to a fork's touch. Remove the disks and set them aside on a cookie sheet.

3. Mix the flour, confectioners' sugar, and a pinch of the allspice in a bowl.

4. In a food processor, place the pistachios, oatmeal, panko, sweet bread crumbs, cardamom, and the second pinch of allspice. Pulse the processor on and off until the ingredients are roughly chopped and mixed. Place in a second bowl.

5. Make an egg wash in a third bowl, using the beaten eggs, half-and-half, and vanilla.

6. Take a squash disk, dredge it in the flour mixture, then the egg wash, then the nut/breading mixture, then set the disk on a cookie sheet. Repeat the process for each disk.

7. Melt the butter in a cast-iron skillet, and place as many disks as will fit in the pan. Fry over medium heat, turning once, until golden brown on each side. Repeat until all the squash disks are fried.

8. Place the fried squash disks on plates lightly sprinkled with confectioners' sugar. Blend the mascarpone cheese with the honey and lavender (you may use ice cream or whipped cream as a topping instead). Top the squash with a scoop of the mascarpone mixture and add a spoonful of ground cherries on the side. Serves 4–6.

BECKY'S BREAD PUDDING

BECKY'S DINER, PORTLAND, ME

Often considered a convenient way to make use of bread that's going stale, bread pudding is actually a versatile and flavorful dessert dish that's done in a variety of ways around the world. Here's the version that Becky's Diner serves up in classic New England style, with cinnamon, nutmeg, and raisins supplying an alluring mixture of flavors and aromas. Stale bread never tasted better!

4	eggs
6	cups whole milk
½	teaspoon salt
1	teaspoon nutmeg
½	tablespoon cinnamon
1½	cups sugar
1	cup raisins
½	loaf stale sandwich bread, cut into slices or 1-inch squares

Preheat the oven to 350°F. Mix all the ingredients except the bread together in a large bowl. Grease a 9 x 13-inch baking pan, and place the bread pieces evenly across the bottom. Pour the contents of the bowl over the bread pieces. Bake for 1 hour, or until the pudding is firm, set, and browned on top. Serves 6.

BUDDHA'S CHOCOLATE

EVELYN'S DRIVE IN, TIVERTON, RI

This crunchy, nutty, toffee-like treat goes great with coffee, tea, or a nice glass of wine. It's appropriate for a snack or as a sweet dessert. Evelyn's co-owner Jane Bitto came up with this recipe, and she warns that Buddha's Chocolate may become habit forming. There's quite a bit of work involved, but for chocolate lovers especially, it's worth it!

1	cup (2 sticks, 8 ounces) butter, softened
1⅓	cups sugar
1	tablespoon light corn syrup
3	tablespoons water
1	cup almonds, finely chopped and divided
1	cup almonds, coarsely chopped
2	8-ounce Hershey's chocolate bars

1. In a medium-heavy pan, combine the butter, sugar, corn syrup, and water. Cook over medium heat, stirring occasionally. When the sugar mixture reaches 280°F on a candy thermometer, stir in the cup of coarsely chopped almonds. Continue to cook/stir the candy mixture until it reaches 300°F. Remove from the heat and spread on a 9 x 13-inch cookie sheet (nonstick works best). Cool thoroughly.

2. Once cooled, loosen the hard candy on the cookie sheet. Melt one bar of chocolate in a saucepan, spread it evenly over the sheet of hard candy, and sprinkle ½ cup of the finely chopped almonds on top. Cool thoroughly again.

3. Slip or flip the candy onto another cookie sheet. Melt the second bar of chocolate in a saucepan, spread evenly over the hard candy, and sprinkle ½ cup of the coarsely chopped almonds on top. Cool thoroughly a third time.

4. Once completely cooled, the candy can be broken into 1-inch-square pieces and stored in a covered container in a cool, dry area. Makes 20–24 pieces of candy.

Pies, Cakes, and Other Baked Goodies

A slice of pie and a cup of coffee is what diner life is all about. New England's diners have come up with some amazing pie recipes over the years, and this chapter has half a dozen excellent ones, along with two great piecrust recipes.

Moody's Diner in Maine and the Agawam Diner north of Boston have built their reputations on award-winning pies. From Moody's, you can try your hand at their recipes for Four-Berry Pie and Walnut Pie. The Agawam is represented here with their recipe for Coconut Cream Pie, and the A1 and Chelsea Royal diners also have entries in the pie category.

Cakes and muffins are well represented, with three cake recipe offerings from Becky's Diner in Portland, and wonderful muffin offerings from the Maine Diner and Moody's. There's also a recipe for the classic New England Johnny Cake, which can be found in a number of New England's finest, most authentic diners.

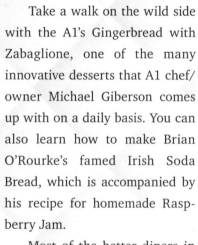

Take a walk on the wild side with the A1's Gingerbread with Zabaglione, one of the many innovative desserts that A1 chef/owner Michael Giberson comes up with on a daily basis. You can also learn how to make Brian O'Rourke's famed Irish Soda Bread, which is accompanied by his recipe for homemade Raspberry Jam.

Most of the better diners in New England do their own baking, and this chapter dishes on 16 wonderful pies, cakes, and baked goodies that you can try at home.

MOM'S PIECRUST

MOODY'S DINER, WALDOBORO, ME

Moody's Diner is known far and wide for the amazing quality and variety of its pies, and one of the reasons is the sinfully rich piecrust that forms the basis of virtually every pie that comes out of Moody's vast bakery operation in their cavernous kitchen.

The "Mom" in Mom's Piecrust refers to Bertha Moody, who founded Moody's Diner back in the 1930s with her husband, Percy, as an add-on to their cabin rental business. Bertha initially did most of the baking in her own kitchen, and she created a number of recipes for the pies that are still on Moody's menu today.

Bertha also developed a recipe for piecrust that has stood the test of time. Though relatively simple to make, it does take some practice to get it just right. The key ingredient is lard, a fairly major no-no in today's culinary culture. However, as with many things in the cooking world, moderation is the key. So, treat yourself to this fabulous crust from time to time, and be sure to stop by Moody's and try the real thing if you have the chance.

1	heaping cup of lard (shortening may be substituted, but it won't be quite as flavorful)
3	cups all-purpose flour
1	teaspoon salt
¾	cup cold water

1. In a large bowl, combine the flour and salt. Cut the lard into the dry ingredients until the mixture resembles coarse cornmeal. Add the water a little at a time until the dough just holds together. (Adding too much water will make the dough tough.)

2. Divide the dough into 2 pieces, the one for the bottom pastry slightly larger than the other. Roll one piece of the dough in a circular pattern on a sheet of flour-sprinkled wax paper. Invert the pastry over a 9-inch standard pie pan, center, and peel off the paper. Gently tuck the pastry into the pan. Repeat. Makes 2 double-crust pies.

MOODY'S FOUR-BERRY PIE

MOODY'S DINER, WALDOBORO, ME

This is perhaps Moody's best-known pie and one of their most popular. It's caused customers to detour far out of their way just to have a slice. To really do it right, be sure to make your pie shell using Bertha Moody's lard-laden piecrust recipe, an excellent crust for this and any other pie you plan to bake (see Mom's Piecrust, page 188).

The four berries (strawberries, blackberries, blueberries, and raspberries) are best when they're fresh, but don't hesitate to use frozen ones as substitutes if fresh ones are out of season or unavailable.

1 cup strawberries	1 cup sugar
1 cup blackberries	2 tablespoons tapioca
1 cup blueberries (Maine blueberries are best, according to Moody's bakers)	Pinch of salt
	½ teaspoon cinnamon
1 cup raspberries	Butter
2 9-inch refrigerated piecrusts (see Mom's Piecrust, page 188)	

Preheat the oven to 350°F. Lightly moisten the rim of one pie shell. Place the berries into the shell. In a small bowl, mix together the sugar, tapioca, salt, and cinnamon, and pour it over the berries. Dot the top with pats of butter. Drape the other pastry over the filling, pressing the top and bottom pastries together along the edge. Trim the pastry flush with the edge of the pan. Using the back of a fork, press the tines along the edge to seal the pastry. Bake for 1 hour, until the top is golden brown. Serves 6.

GINGERBREAD WITH ZABAGLIONE

A1 DINER, GARDINER, ME

The first thing you should notice about this recipe for gingerbread is that it has no ginger in it. The nutmeg, cinnamon, and cloves combine for a unique ginger-like flavor. This recipe calls for a 9 x 13-inch cake pan, which will provide more than enough gingerbread for the zabaglione. You may set aside half of the gingerbread and snack on it whenever you wish. Slice the other half into squares, which will receive the zabaglione topping—a recipe that will challenge your culinary skills, but it's very rich and distinctive, with its dollop of sweet marsala wine, and well worth the time and effort involved.

GINGERBREAD

- ½ cup sugar
- ½ teaspoon salt
- 2 teaspoons baking soda
- ½ teaspoon nutmeg
- 1 teaspoon cinnamon
- ¼ teaspoon ground cloves
- 2 eggs
- 1 cup molasses
- ½ cup vegetable oil or melted shortening
- 2½ cups all-purpose flour
- ½ cup hot water

ZABAGLIONE

- 6 egg yolks, room temperature
- ⅝ cup granulated white sugar
- ⅓ cup all-purpose flour
- 2 cups milk
- 3 tablespoons marsala wine
- 1 cup heavy cream (whipping cream may be substituted)

1. To make the gingerbread, preheat the oven to 350°F. Grease a 9 x 13-inch cake pan. In a small bowl, mix together the sugar, salt, baking soda, nutmeg, cinnamon, and cloves. In a large bowl, beat the eggs with the molasses. Add the vegetable oil or melted shortening and the flour to the eggs and molasses mixture and stir to combine.

2. Add the sugar-and-spice mixture to the large bowl, and stir to combine all ingredients. Slowly add enough hot water to make a thin batter. Pour the batter into the pan, and bake for 20–25 minutes or until a cake tester or toothpick comes out clean.

3. To make the zabaglione, in a saucepan, mix all the ingredients except the cream. Blend them well. Whisk this mixture over medium heat, just until it starts to boil. This should take 12–15 minutes.

4. Transfer the mixture to a medium-size bowl. Place the bowl in a larger bowl of ice water and whisk until chilled to a custard-like consistency. Whip the cream in a separate bowl until it's stiff, and then fold it into the custard. Dollop spoonfuls of the zabaglione onto individual squares of the gingerbread. Serves approximately 6–8. Save the leftover gingerbread for snacking.

"When I Get Hungry . . . I Get Moody"

✕ 1885 Atlantic Highway
   Waldoboro, ME 04572

☎ 207-832-7785

ⓘ www.moodysdiner.com

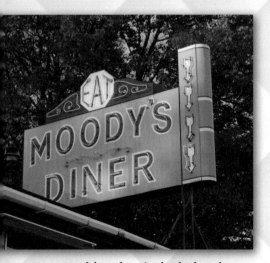

Moody's rooftop sign has beckoned customers along US Route 1 for decades.

Moody's Diner

So says the slogan on one of the T-shirts for sale in the gift shop next to Moody's Diner in Waldoboro, Maine. Few, if any, diners in America have the extensive family history that this place does. Moody's has been around in one form or another since 1927, when Percy and Bertha Moody opened a few small cabins for rent on their hilltop property. Today, with third-, fourth-, and even fifth-generation family members (about 20 or so Moody relations, total) working in the business, Moody's is the epitome of a family business run the right way.

A few years after those first cabins opened in the 1920s, Percy and Bertha opened a small restaurant, which they called the Tea Room, to serve hungry guests who didn't want to go into town for a meal. Percy also purchased a lunch wagon (a precursor to diners as we know them today), and he began selling hot dogs and other victuals by the roadside. In 1934, US 1 was rerouted to the north of Moody's, so the enterprising Moody family purchased land along the new route and built and opened what is known today as Moody's Diner. Current general manager and third-generation Moody family member Dan Beck estimates that since Moody's Diner opened on US 1 in the 1930s, the building has been expanded upon or remodeled at least 20 times.

Moody's is truly massive for a diner. From the highway, it looks more like a roadhouse, and it can seat over a hundred hungry patrons at a time. Upon entering the diner you're confronted with a long, well-worn counter with more than a dozen swiveling stools in front and dessert display cases above and behind the service area. This counter section is in the spot of the original 1934 diner that popped up on US 1. Off to the right in the expansive dining room are numerous booths and tables. The walls are lined with Moody's memorabilia—historic photographs of the diner's evolution over the years, awards that the diner has won, and lots of propaganda promoting Moxie, a soft drink that's popular with Moody's regular customers.

The menu is 100 percent diner fare. Start with the breakfasts. There are all the standard variations on eggs, bacon/sausage, homefries, and toast, as well as pancakes (get them with Maine blueberries if they're available), waffles, award-winning blueberry muffins, and homemade, fried-in-lard doughnuts that are sinfully good. The homemade corned beef hash is also not to be missed.

For lunch, all the usual sandwich suspects are available, plus lobster, clam, and Maine shrimp rolls. Perhaps the best and most alluring midday meal at Moody's is the black angus burger, served in quarter- and half-pound sizes. Try the Percy Burger, named after the founder. It's a hefty half-pounder topped with grilled mushrooms and melted Swiss cheese. All these sandwich selections go great with a Hamilton Beach–mixed milk shake or a cold bottle of Moxie.

The daily specials are served from 11 am until they're gone, and they're straight-up diner fare at its finest. Throughout the week you can choose from such classics as Yankee Pot Roast, Meat Loaf (see page 95), Turkey Pot Pie, New England Boiled Dinner, Baked Stuffed Haddock, Smothered Beef and Onions, and Roast Turkey or Pork, which are served on alternating Sundays. You may also wish to try the seafood, which comes in a variety of deep-fried platters for the most part. The seafood is super fresh and very affordably priced. There aren't many places where you can get a full-on seafood platter for less than $20, and Moody's delivers on both quality and value in this category.

Regulars at Moody's will tell you that the primary reason to come to the diner is for its home-baked pies. The lard-laden recipe for Moody's piecrust dates back

Moody's lengthy counter and cavernous dining room can pack 'em in.

to Bertha Moody's days of baking pies in the oven of the Moody home before they expanded the kitchen at the diner to accommodate their baking needs. If you ever get the chance to glimpse into the diner's enormous kitchen, you'll see a large area devoted to assembling and baking nothing but pies.

At any given time, Moody's menu advertises about a dozen different pie offerings. The most popular one, according to a survey of regulars conducted by Moody's at a customer appreciation event, is Chocolate Cream Pie. The most famous ones, however, are Moody's Four-Berry Pie and Walnut Pie (see pages 189 and 204). Each has won accolades in the national press on numerous occasions.

And what's good pie without good coffee? Moody's gets theirs in bulk from New England Coffee, a high-quality, Massachusetts-based purveyor. So, be sure to have a slice and a cup before hitting the highway on your way to Rockland or Acadia or Down East Maine. Moody's is your last, best diner choice between Mid-Coast Maine and the Canadian border.

BECKY'S BLUEBERRY CAKE

BECKY'S DINER, PORTLAND, ME

Blueberries and Maine are like Astaire and Rogers—natural partners that go very well together. The Pine Tree State has a special relationship with the little blue guys, especially the more tart version that grows in the northern reaches of Maine and that you'll find fresh in all sorts of summertime Maine dishes, from pancakes to muffins to salads and desserts.

For this recipe, you can use any type of blueberry you wish—even frozen ones—so you can enjoy this fine, two-layered cake any time of year. Regardless of the blueberry type or the season, Becky's Blueberry Cake will bring a little bit of summertime into your home.

CAKE

4–5	cups fresh or frozen blueberries
4	eggs, separated
2¼	cups sugar, divided
1	cup shortening
½	teaspoon salt
2	teaspoons vanilla extract
3	cups all-purpose flour, plus more for dusting
2	teaspoons baking powder
⅔	cup milk

CREAM CHEESE FROSTING

1	cup (2 sticks, 8 ounces) butter
2	cups cream cheese
2	teaspoons vanilla extract
2–2½	cups confectioners' sugar

1. To make the cake, preheat the oven to 350°F. Thaw and/or drain the blueberries, dust lightly with flour, and set aside. Separate the egg whites and yolks into small bowls. Add ¼ cup of the sugar to the egg whites and beat until stiff. Set aside.

2. In a large bowl, mix together the remaining 2 cups of sugar and the shortening. Add the salt, vanilla, and egg yolks, and stir. Then add the flour, baking powder, and milk, and mix well. Fold in the stiffened egg whites, then gently fold in the lightly floured blueberries.

3. Grease 2 round cake pans and dust them with flour. Pour half of the batter into each pan. Bake for 50–60 minutes, until the center springs back when gently pressed or a cake tester or toothpick comes out clean.

4. To make the frosting, mix all the ingredients in a mixer until smooth, then spread the frosting over the cake layers once they're completely cooled. Serves 8–10.

CORN MUFFINS

MAINE DINER, WELLS, ME

One of the most popular items at the Maine Diner, be it at breakfast, lunch, or dinner, are the corn muffins that come hot out of the oven all day long. Essentially a Johnny Cake disguised as a muffin, these tasty morsels are quick and easy to make. (They're also flavor-enhanced with a bit of bacon grease added to the mix before baking.)

¾	cup cornmeal
1	cup all-purpose flour
3	teaspoons baking powder
⅓	cup sugar
¾	teaspoon salt
1	cup milk
1	egg, well beaten
2	teaspoons melted bacon fat

Preheat the oven to 425°F. Sift and mix together the cornmeal, flour, baking powder, sugar, and salt. Once they're well blended, stir in the milk, egg, and bacon fat and continue mixing until well blended. Pour the mixture into a greased muffin pan, and bake for 20–25 minutes, until the muffin tops are golden. Makes 4 large or 6 medium muffins.

BLUEBERRY MUFFINS

MOODY'S DINER, WALDOBORO, ME

Any dyed-in-the-wool Mainer will tell you that blueberry muffins are best with the more tart Maine strain of blueberries. Moody's Diner harvests most of its in-season Maine blueberries from farms right in town, so they're super fresh.

Truth be told, you can use any sort of blueberry (including frozen) in Moody's version of down-home blueberry muffins, and they'll taste great regardless of the berry source. Moody's blueberry muffins, by the way, earned a gold medal from the Culinary Hall of Fame a number of years ago.

- 6 cups all-purpose flour, plus more for dusting
- 4 tablespoons baking powder
- 1½ teaspoons salt
- 1 cup sugar
- 3 eggs
- 3 cups milk
- 1 cup shortening, melted
- 2 cups blueberries

Preheat the oven to 400°F. In a small bowl, mix together the flour, baking powder, salt, and sugar. Set aside. Beat the eggs in a large bowl, add the milk, and blend in the dry ingredients. Add the melted shortening and mix some more. Dust the blueberries with some flour and fold them into the batter. Fill greased muffin tins ¾ full. Bake for 20 minutes. Makes 10–12 muffins.

A Green Mountains Roadside Delight

✕ 487 Marlboro Road
    West Brattleboro, VT 05303

☎ 802-254-8399

① www.chelsearoyaldiner.com

Chelsea Royal Diner

Southern Vermont serves as a gateway of sorts to this verdant state, and in the town of West Brattleboro there's a pleasant anomaly nestled against the Green Mountains: an old-time diner with a long history in the area.

The Chelsea Royal Diner was a culinary mainstay in the city of Brattleboro for decades until it moved one town west on US 9 in the 1970s. The classic 1938 Worcester dining car was grafted onto the front of an existing restaurant, giving the place an appealing diner look from the road and extra seating in the existing restaurant space to the rear.

Around about 1990 Todd Darrah purchased the Chelsea Royal and began slowly shaping it into the type of eatery he felt the area needed and yet lacked at the time. He was an early proponent of using local products and ingredients in his cooking, and to that end he planted an herb and vegetable garden that still supplies the restaurant with all sorts of fresh produce in season. He and partner Janet Picard have also raised livestock on their "back 40" in the form of chickens, turkeys, and pigs. There are numerous farms in the vicinity that supply everything from real maple syrup to Vermont cheddar cheese to fresh bison meat.

The Chelsea Diner's menu

Chelsea Royal's nicely appointed counter by the kitchen.

is an eclectic mix of regular diner fare, fresh vegetable dishes, and a smattering of Mexican and other southwestern selections. Breakfast features an interesting range of omelets stuffed with all sorts of meats and veggies, a popular Cajun Breakfast Skillet (see page 22), and giant, home-baked cinnamon buns that disappear pretty quickly once the morning crowd starts to arrive.

The heart of the Chelsea Royal Diner is this classic 1938 Worcester dining car.

In terms of ambience and atmosphere, the Chelsea Royal excels in coziness and diner good vibes. You may grab a booth in the old diner section up front or one of the booths nearer the kitchen in the original restaurant portion, where you may admire some of Janet's impressionistic paintings of the diner and surrounding gardens that hang on the walls. There's a counter (not the original one that came with the diner car) that has about half a dozen stools in the restaurant portion facing the kitchen where breakfast pastries are on display and black-and-white tile work enhances the diner atmosphere.

All this is kept light and fun by a cheerful, experienced service staff, many of whom have been waiting tables, booths, and the six-stool counter at Chelsea Royal for years. They're extremely helpful at filling customers in on what looks good in the kitchen, oftentimes the daily

The diner's famous burger, made from locally raised, grass-fed beef.

specials that are cooked up on a revolving schedule and listed on a blackboard.

One last thing to note about this southern Vermont charmer: it's one of the only diners anywhere to have its own homemade ice cream stand. The little service window on the front of the building next to the diner car is open from April to October, and Janet oversees the making of more than a dozen different ice cream flavors from scratch. So, order up a dish or a cone, grab a seat at one of the picnic tables out front, or stroll around back to check out Chelsea Royal's gardens. From your first cup of coffee in the morning until your last scoop of ice cream at night, Chelsea Royal is the place to dine in this charming corner of Vermont.

MAPLE WALNUT PIE

CHELSEA ROYAL DINER, WEST BRATTLEBORO, VT

In Vermont, there's no substitute for real maple syrup, and that's a closely followed rule at Vermont's Chelsea Royal Diner. Locally harvested maple syrup is a key ingredient in their Maple Walnut Pie, and you're going to want to use the real thing when you bake this pie up at home. This is a relatively simple pie to make, since it doesn't involve procuring or slicing up fruit or vegetables; and it's awfully rich and sweet, making it a favorite of kids as well as dessert-loving adults.

1	cup walnuts
1	9-inch refrigerated piecrust
1¼	cups 100 percent pure Vermont maple syrup
2	tablespoons (¼ stick, 1 ounce) butter
½	cup brown sugar
2	tablespoons all-purpose flour
3	eggs
1	teaspoon vanilla extract

Preheat the oven to 350°F. Place the walnuts in the pie shell. In a saucepan or small pot, heat the maple syrup, butter, and brown sugar until steaming, then reduce to a simmer. Whisk in the flour. Whip the eggs and vanilla in a separate bowl. Slowly add the heated syrup mixture to the eggs and vanilla and stir until well blended. Pour the mixture on top of the walnuts. Bake for approximately 45 minutes. Let cool. Serves 4–6.

PUMPKIN BREAD

MAINE DINER, WELLS, ME

There are all sorts of things you can do with pumpkins after harvest in the fall, and pumpkin bread is one of the better choices. You may, of course, use canned pumpkin to equal effect and make pumpkin bread any time of year. (Lots of cooks actually prefer the canned version, as it's much easier to work with and in many opinions every bit as flavorful.) A warm slice of this bread slathered in butter, honey, or your favorite jam is a welcome snack or side.

3⅓	cups all-purpose flour
2	teaspoons baking soda
3	cups sugar
1½	teaspoons salt
1	teaspoon nutmeg
2	cups pumpkin flesh, mashed (canned pumpkin works just as well)
1	cup vegetable oil
4	eggs
⅔	cup water

Preheat the oven to 350°F. Grease two 5 x 9-inch bread loaf pans. Put the flour, baking soda, sugar, salt, and nutmeg in a large bowl. Add the pumpkin, oil, eggs, and water. Beat thoroughly with a broad, stout spoon. Pour equal amounts into the loaf pans and bake for 55–60 minutes. Let cool, then remove from bake pans and slice. Serves 8–10.

CARROT CAKE

BECKY'S DINER, PORTLAND, ME

Carrot cake at its best is equal parts healthy and sinful, and the Becky's Diner version is no exception. This recipe calls for a mountain of shredded carrots and a healthy helping of chopped walnuts, counterbalanced by generous amounts of sugar and eggs. The end result is Becky's Carrot Cake, a rich, dense, flavorful cake that looks as good as it tastes.

CAKE

4	eggs
1	cup salad oil
5	cups shredded carrots
2	cups all-purpose flour
2	cups sugar
2	teaspoons baking soda
1	teaspoon salt
2	teaspoons cinnamon
½	teaspoon nutmeg
2	cups walnuts, chopped

CREAM CHEESE FROSTING

1	cup (2 sticks, 8 ounces) butter
2	cups cream cheese
2	teaspoons vanilla extract
2–2½	cups confectioners' sugar

1. To make the cake, preheat the oven to 350°F. In a large bowl, mix the eggs, salad oil, and shredded carrots. Then add the flour, sugar, baking soda, salt, cinnamon, nutmeg, and walnuts. Mix until smooth. Pour the batter mixture into two greased, round cake pans. Bake for 30–35 minutes or until the center springs back to the touch or when a cake tester or toothpick comes out clean.

2. To make the frosting, mix in a mixer until smooth. Spread over the carrot cake layers once they are completely cooled. Serves 8–10.

MOODY'S WALNUT PIE

MOODY'S DINER, WALDOBORO, ME

The biggest selling item at Moody's is pie, and their walnut pie is one of the most famous and popular pies to come out of their ovens. This pie has the sweetness and consistency of a good pecan pie, and it's every bit as satisfying. Be sure to make your crust using Mom's Piecrust recipe (see page 188), Bertha Moody's time-tested, flaky piecrust and the recipe for which she is perhaps best known.

¾ cup (1½ sticks, 6 ounces) margarine, melted

1½ cups sugar

9 eggs

3 heaping tablespoons all-purpose flour

¾ teaspoon salt

1½ teaspoons vanilla extract

2½ cups dark corn syrup

2 cups milk

2 cups walnuts, chopped and divided

2 9-inch piecrusts (see Mom's Piecrust, page 188)

Preheat the oven to 350°F. In a large bowl, beat together the melted margarine, sugar, eggs, flour, salt, vanilla, and corn syrup, then stir in the milk. Spread 1 cup of the chopped walnuts into each pie shell. Pour the batter over the nuts. Bake for 30–40 minutes. Serves 10–12.

JOHNNY CAKE

MOODY'S DINER, WALDOBORO, ME

This New England staple dates back at least a couple of centuries and may be served as either a side dish, like cornbread or biscuits, or as a meal onto itself. (Breakfast would probably be most appropriate.) This recipe calls for baking up Johnny Cake in a large baking pan, though individual-size Johnny Cakes can be made as muffins from the same recipe.

2	cups all-purpose flour
1½	tablespoons baking powder
1½	cups cornmeal
½	teaspoon salt
1	cup sugar
2	eggs
¾	cup vegetable oil
2½	cups milk

Preheat the oven to 350°F. Sift the flour, baking powder, cornmeal, salt, and sugar together. Beat the eggs in a separate bowl and add to the dry ingredients. Mix well, then add the oil. Mix again, then add the milk. Stir together and pour the batter into a greased 9 x 12-inch baking dish. Bake for 1 hour. Serves 12.

A Diner Family Dynasty

✕ 166 Newburyport Turnpike
Rowley, MA 01969

☎ 978-948-7780

Agawam Diner

The Agawam Diner's 70-plus-year history is long and complicated—and very interesting, if you can follow it. Since 1940, the Galanis and Pappas families between them have owned four diners in places as scattered as Ipswich, Massachusetts; Brunswick, Maine; Peabody, Massachusetts; and the current Agawam Diner at the intersection of US 1 and 133 in Rowley, Massachusetts. Countless mothers, fathers, sons, daughters, cousins, and grandchildren have worked in the family business over the decades, and it doesn't look like that will change any time soon. (When you visit the Agawam, be sure to read the diner's complex and colorful history on the back of the menu.)

Current times find the extended families still running the Agawam in its shiny, stainless-steel Fodero dining car building, with its handsome red awning covering the front entrance. You may verify the diner's provenance by checking out the little plaque, installed by the Fodero Dining Car Company in 1954, that sits above a door in the diner. This is one of two Foderos that the family purchased that year. The building was added to the National Register of Historic Places in 1999.

If you word-associate with anyone who lives within a 50-mile radius of the diner and say "Agawam," chances are every respondent will say "pie." The Agawam is famous for its pies, and co-owner and head baker Bubba

The Agawam Diner's pedigree as an authentic 1950s Fodero dining car.

The Agawam's distinctive stainless steel skin shimmers day and night.

Galanis puts up as many as 40 pies every day in the diner's back-room baking area. There are glass cases at each end of the counter in the dining room that are filled with the day's offerings of pies and other home-baked desserts.

On any given day, you'll be able to choose between 8 to 12 different types of pies. There are the usual apple, blueberry, strawberry, raspberry, and pumpkin pies, along with a dizzying array of cream pie varieties: banana, coconut, chocolate, and lemon meringue. Whipped cream is used in abundance on every pie slice, unless you tell them that you'd like to abstain. If it's available the day you're there, give serious consideration to a slice of angel pie—a dreamy combination of vanilla custard and chocolate cake baked into a piecrust and topped with whipped cream. It should come as no surprise that it's a local favorite.

Pie is the reason most people come to the Agawam Diner— again and again.

Before diving into dessert, treat yourself to some of the most authentic 1950s-style diner food you'll find anywhere. The Agawam's standard diner dishes, such as meat loaf, liver and onions, the hot open-faced turkey sandwich, and Chicken Pie (served upside down; see page 92) are perfectly prepared, abundant in their portion sizes, and more than affordable. Weekly dinner specials include such entrées as chicken croquettes, braised bourbon-marinated turkey tips, baked haddock, tender lamb shank, and roast pork, each served with all the trimmings.

One special entrée to try at the Agawam is the fried clam plate. The recipe for these wonderfully delectable morsels is shared with the Clam Box seafood stand in nearby Ipswich. "The Box" is owned by Marina "Chickie" Aggelakis, whose father was one of the founders of the Agawam Diner. The fried clams at the Clam Box, and by extension the Agawam, are arguably the best fried clams in the world.

The sweet, crunchy breading is achieved through the use of corn flour, pastry flour, and evaporated milk in just the right quantities. The clams are then fried in super-pure cooking oil, and the end result is heavenly. (One of the best things about New England diners is that they all tend to have great seafood.)

Breakfast and lunch at the Agawam are pretty straightforward. The omelets are massive and loaded with whatever meat, veggie, or hash you desire to have folded in and cooked up within. Lots of people love the fried chicken at lunchtime, as well as the country-fried steak smothered in gravy. The burgers, although on the small side, are very nicely prepared and more than affordable.

The Agawam is an efficient powerhouse of a diner that serves as an example of how to run a diner, or any restaurant, correctly. With all the family members currently involved at the Agawam and all the others waiting in the wings, this place should prosper for a long time to come. Hats off to the Galanis and Pappas families for making the Agawam so special.

PIECRUST

AGAWAM DINER, ROWLEY, MA

The Agawam Diner is up there in the diner pantheon when it comes to pies. Chef-owner John "Bubba" Galanis makes up to 40 pies each day in his on-the-premises bakery, many of which are sold as whole pies to local customers, who take them home and savor every bite with family and friends.

Here's Bubba's recipe for piecrust, which can, of course, be applied to any pie you wish to bake.

- 1 cup pastry flour
- 1 tablespoon powdered milk
- 1 teaspoon salt
- ⅔ cup vegetable shortening
- 3 tablespoons water

1. Preheat the oven to 400°F. Whisk the flour, powdered milk, and salt together in a bowl. Work the shortening in with your hands until marble-size lumps form. Do not overmix, as the crust won't firm up properly when formed and baked. Make an indentation in the top of the dough ball and pour in 3 tablespoons of water. Dig your fingers into the dough and pull it up and over the indentation without squeezing, until a soft dough forms. Pat the dough into a five-inch disk shape, and transfer it to a lightly floured counter or other surface.

2. Roll the dough into an 11-inch-wide circle, and transfer it to a 10-inch greased or disposable aluminum pie pan. Press the dough against the edges of the pan, pressing together any tears that may occur in the process. Trim away any dough that extends over the edge of the pan.

3. Place another 10-inch pie pan inside, sandwiching the dough between the pans, and press down gently. Bake the pie shell sandwich upside down on a baking sheet for 20–25 minutes, until golden brown. Remove from the oven and let it cool. Finally, invert the pie sandwich and remove the top pan. Makes 1 piecrust.

COCONUT CREAM PIE

AGAWAM DINER, ROWLEY, MA

Of the many different types of pies that come out of the Agawam's bakery, one of the finest is the Coconut Cream Pie. This cream-covered colossus is almost as pleasing to the eye as it is to the palate. The Agawam's recipe for this pie appeared in *Saveur* magazine a while back, and here it is for you to try at home.

5⅓ cups milk, divided

1⅓ cups sugar

½ cup corn starch

6 eggs

Pinch of salt

1 cup sweetened coconut flakes (1 tablespoon of them lightly pan-toasted)

1 9-inch refrigerated piecrust

1 2.6-ounce container Dream Whip whipped topping mix

1. Bring 4⅓ cups of milk to a boil in a medium pot over medium-high heat. At the same time, whisk together the sugar, corn starch, eggs, and salt in a large bowl. Drizzle the hot milk into the egg mixture, whisking constantly.

2. Return the mixture to the pot and cook over medium heat, stirring constantly until very thick, which should take approximately 15–17 minutes. Fold in the untoasted coconut flakes. Transfer the mixture to a large bowl, cover with plastic wrap or a tight-fitting lid, and let cool to room temperature.

3. Transfer the cooled mixture into the pie shell. Put the whipped topping mix and the cup of remaining milk into a large bowl, and beat to stiff peaks. (You may alternatively use sweetened whipped cream, but it won't hold up as long on top of the pie.)

4. Transfer the topping to a pastry bag fitted with a star tip and pipe the topping onto the pie in three rows, zig-zagging to create swirls. Sprinkle the toasted coconut over the top. Chill the pie in a refrigerator for 3–4 hours. Serves 8.

LEMON COCONUT PIE

A1 DINER, GARDINER, ME

Mike Giberson, the co-owner and head chef at the A1 Diner, always seems to come up with pleasant twists and variations on standard recipes. This pie combines the disparate flavors of lemon and coconut with a splash of buttermilk for an unusual and uniquely light yet substantial pie.

½ cup (1 stick, 4 ounces) butter, at room temperature

2 cups granulated white sugar

4 large eggs

⅔ cup buttermilk

1 teaspoon vanilla extract

2 tablespoons lemon juice

2 teaspoons lemon zest

1 cup shredded coconut, plus 4 tablespoons

1 9-inch refrigerated piecrust

1. Preheat the oven to 350°F. In the bowl of an electric mixer, cream the butter and sugar until light and fluffy. Add the eggs one at a time, beating until pale yellow and creamy. Add the buttermilk, vanilla, and lemon juice, beating until well combined. Add the lemon zest.

2. Stir in 1 cup of the coconut, then pour the filling into the pie shell. Sprinkle the rest of the coconut on top of the pie and bake for 45 minutes, until the top of the pie is browned. Serves 8–10.

GERMAN CHOCOLATE CAKE

BECKY'S DINER, PORTLAND, ME

This cake is a chocolate lover's dream.

1	package (½ cup) German sweet chocolate
½	cup water
1	cup (2 sticks, 8 ounces) butter, softened
2	cups sugar
4	eggs, yolks and whites separated
1	teaspoon vanilla extract
2	cups all-purpose flour
1	teaspoon baking soda
¼	teaspoon salt
1	cup buttermilk

1. Preheat the oven to 350°F. Melt the chocolate in a microwave oven, using a small bowl sitting in a larger bowl with water in it, until melted (1.5–2 minutes). Make sure the bowls are microwave safe. Set aside.

2. In a separate mixing bowl, beat the butter and sugar until fluffy, then add the egg yolks and beat together. Blend in the chocolate and vanilla. Add the flour, baking soda, and salt, alternating with portions of the buttermilk.

3. In a separate bowl, beat the egg whites until stiff. Gently fold these into the mixing bowl. Pour the batter into two buttered, floured 9-inch round cake pans. Bake for 30 minutes or until centers spring back when pressed gently or a cake tester or toothpick comes out clean. Serves 10–12.

Hermit Crab Diners

Hermit crabs are known for periodically scouring the ocean floor in search of empty seashells to occupy and make into their new homes. The crab gets a new place to live (along with protection from predators), and the shell attains a new purpose.

In the same vein, disused diners sometimes get taken over by a restaurant that's not a diner. The diner building is typically refurbished to its former glory, and it reopens with a new lease on life, albeit not as a diner. Such is the case with a couple of hermit crab diners in New England. One of them is an Indian restaurant, and the other serves Thai food. Both are excellent examples of how diners can reinvent themselves and continue to bring joy (and good food) to the neighborhoods where they're located.

Tandoor, the Clay Oven restaurant found a home in this 1950s Mountain View Diner.

Tandoor, the Clay Oven

1226 Chapel Street, New Haven, CT 06457
203-776-6620
www.tandoornewhaven.com

Right in the middle of New Haven's bustling downtown district and not too far from the Yale University campus sits a vintage 1955 Mountain View diner that serves nary a bit of diner food these days. Back in the 1990s the diner was turned into Tandoor, the Clay Oven, an Indian restaurant catering to the area's high demand for quality South Asian cuisine. All the standard Indian dishes, such as chicken tikka masala, lamb curry, and tandoori chicken are featured, along with dozens of other dishes from various regions around India. Much of the better menu choices are cooked in a large clay oven, as are all the naan breads. The diner still retains many of its original features, like polished wood trim, stainless steel panels and backsplashes, and original tile work in many places. If you're a fan of Indian food and diners, this is a place you should definitely check out.

There's no diner food on the menu at Tandoor—just top-knotch Indian cuisine.

Lanna Thai Diner

901c Main Street
Woburn, MA 01801
781-932-0394
www.lannathaidiner.com

There's a small Worcester diner car just a bit north of I-495 in the northwest Boston suburb of Woburn that went Thai in the early 2000s, and it has received very favorable reviews for both its food and its preservation of many of the diner's original features. There's good reason for the preservation: the diner is on the National Register of Historic Places, albeit under one of its previous names—Jack's Diner. Current owner Agachai "Max" Katong has done an excellent job of transforming the tiny eatery into a popular Thai restaurant that can seat only a couple dozen customers at a time. (No doubt his carryout business helps him keep afloat financially.) Max hails from northern Thailand, and dishes such as nam prik ong and purple sticky rice, which are popular in his part of Thailand, appear alongside more familiar dishes like pad thai, gyoza, satay, and red curry. The dining room is a charming mix of American and Thai, with original chrome, wood paneling, and tile work, alongside such features as four carved wooden cats swathed in silk scarves. Dining at Lanna Thai brings together East and West in a warm and wonderful way, and it helps save and preserve a classic diner car at the same time.

Lanna Thai Diner is housed in a diminutive Worcester dining car.

Lanna Thai has lovingly restored the diner's interior—with a few Thai touches thrown in.

A carved wooden cat draped in silk and wearing a feathered hat greets customers by the door.

IRISH SODA BREAD

O'ROURKE'S DINER, MIDDLETOWN, CT

Brian O'Rourke is constantly baking many different types of breads at his diner, and upon arriving, customers are treated to a small sampling plate of whatever bread was baked up that morning. One of the bread staples at O'Rourke's is Irish Soda Bread, which is served as a side with a number of Irish dishes. This wholesome, raisin-inflected bread is great right out of the oven at home, with some jam or butter and a hot cup of coffee or tea any time of day.

- 2½ cups all-purpose flour
- 1 cup plus 2 tablespoons sugar
- ¼ teaspoon salt
- ½ teaspoon baking soda
- ¼ teaspoon baking powder
- 1 cup raisins (Brian uses golden raisins)
- ½ tablespoon caraway seeds, toasted (optional; toast in a frying pan over medium-high heat for 2–3 minutes or until fragrant)
- 2 eggs, beaten
- ½ cup sour cream
- ⅓ cup vegetable oil
- ⅓ cup buttermilk

1. Preheat the oven to 350°F. Grease a 9 x 5-inch loaf pan. In a medium bowl, whisk together the flour, sugar, salt, baking soda, baking powder, raisins, and caraway seeds. Set aside.

2. Form a well in the center of the dough ball. In a separate bowl, combine the beaten eggs (be sure to beat before adding remaining ingredients), sour cream, oil, and buttermilk. Add the wet ingredients to the dry ingredients, and stir with a wooden spoon or by hand just until combined. Do not overmix. The batter should be thick.

3. Spoon the mixture into the greased pan and quickly put it into the oven. Bake until the bread is golden brown and a knife inserted into the center comes out clean, about 60–75 minutes. Remove the loaf from the oven; let it rest for 10 minutes, then invert the loaf onto a wire rack and cool. Serves 8–10.

Variation: Soak the raisins in Irish whiskey tea overnight for added flavors. Make Irish whiskey tea by adding 2 tablespoons of Irish whiskey to 2 cups of tea.

RASPBERRY JAM

O'ROURKE'S DINER, MIDDLETOWN, CT

Here's an amazingly simple recipe for making your own homemade raspberry jam for spreading on bread, muffins, and other baked goods. It's also got some interesting flavorings in the form of apple, orange, and cinnamon. According to Brian O'Rourke, the difference between jelly and jam is that jelly wiggles while jam sits. True enough. Jam is cooked down and consists of more fruit and less sugar than jelly, giving jam a more stationary demeanor. One you try this quick recipe for raspberry jam, you may never buy another jar of jam from the store again.

- 4   cups frozen raspberries (or fresh, if in season)
- 2   cups sugar
- 2   apples, cored and quartered
- 1   orange, peeled and quartered
- 3   cinnamon sticks
- 1   package fruit pectin (preferably Certo)

Place all the ingredients in a large pan and bring to a simmer for approximately 40 minutes. Let cool and store in jars or other airtight containers and refrigerate. You can also can or freeze the jam and enjoy it weeks or months later. Makes approximately 4 cups of jam.

Acknowledgments

It took nearly a year and a half to research and write this cookbook, and I had plenty of help along the way. I'd like to gratefully acknowledge the following people:

First and foremost, all the owners and chefs who welcomed me into their diners and kitchens and who shared with me dozens of recipes, stories, photographs, and dishes that make this cookbook a comprehensive profile of diner food in New England today. These owners pour a lot of hours and love into their establishments and their culinary craft, and I owe them a debt of gratitude for their participation in this project.

Special thanks to Dick Henry (Maine Diner), Ted Karousos (Blue Plate Diner), Becky Rand (Becky's Diner), Dan Beck (Moody's Diner), Jane and Domenic Bitto (Evelyn's Drive-In), and Brian O'Rourke (O'Rourke's Diner) for the extraordinary number of recipes each contributed to the book. Such generosity will hopefully be rewarded by many curious customers showing up at their diners to discover what the dishes described in this book actually look and taste like when prepared by their originators.

Once again, my friend Fred Liebling gave me shelter during my trips to Maine so that I could explore the amazing diners in that state at a leisurely pace. I owe him my thanks and more than a couple of meals at the diner of his choice.

This book took longer to complete than I ever thought, and I'm grateful to the fine staff at Countryman Press for their patience while I worked the Internet, e-mail, and phone lines and drove throughout the six-state region, gathering information, taking photographs, and assembling the manuscript. Special thanks to editorial director Kermit Hummel, who has enthusiastically supported this project from the beginning; to managing editor Lisa Sacks, who guided the manuscript and hundreds of photos through the book production process like the pro that she is; and to copy editor Abby Collier, whose comments, suggestions, and edits to the manuscript made me look much better in print than I deserve.

I once again had the pleasure of working with my pal Vicky Shea, who created the beautiful design for this book. It's yet one more project where her creative skills have left me speechless and her bonhomie has made the production process a joy.

Finally, thanks to my wife, Ellen, and our four children, Nick, Natalie, Brian, and Max, who supplied support on the home front and who occasionally acted as guinea pigs while I tested various recipes in our home kitchen. If I've instilled in any of them a love of New England diner food, then this has all been well worth it.

—Mike Urban

Index

Featured Diners

The following diners are featured and described in the book, along with their locations and contact information. Pay them a visit—they're special places.